"This is not a book about polar bears,
for 'saving the earth.' It is a book ab
claim 'the human art of creaturely life.' Wirzba shows why creation, incarnation, and redemption are intricately bound up in bodies—our own, other creatures', and the earth's—and why if we're to care for those bodies we need to adopt an 'iconic vision of the world' that only Jesus makes possible. A deeply hopeful book written in prose both artful and lucid, this confirms Norman Wirzba's place as one of the finest theologians writing today."

—**Fred Bahnson**, author of *Soil and Sacrament*; director, Food, Faith, and Religious Leadership Initiative, Wake Forest University School of Divinity

"In a moment when conversations about environmental stewardship have become divisive and polarizing, Wirzba offers a level-headed 'peace; be still.' He reminds Christians that our world was created and is sustained by an intentional Craftsman who has asked us to steward it well. Wirzba's words are fertile soil, fresh air, and a bountiful harvest that will stir your passion for creation and stoke your love for the Creator. This soon-to-be-classic text on the theology of creation has come to us not a moment too soon."

—**Jonathan Merritt**, author of *Jesus Is Better Than You Imagined*; senior columnist at *Religion News Service*

"In this wise, prophetic, and expansive book, Norman Wirzba offers us an extended meditation on creation with compelling eloquence. Here is a theology that is (literally) grounded in the gift of soil. A multidisciplinary treatise expertly engaging philosophy, theology, literature, and ecology, this book moves effortlessly from postmodern theory to agricultural policy, from biblical interpretation to gardening, from economics to a spirituality of gratitude. Wirzba invites us into a world of interdependent intimacy, sympathy, hospitality, delight, and love. This book is a generous gift that bears witness to a world characterized as gift."

—**Brian J. Walsh**, University of Toronto; author of *Kicking at the Darkness: Bruce Cockburn and the Christian Imagination*

"In this brief book, Norman Wirzba casts a profound vision of creaturely life, of what it means to live as creatures within an interconnected creation that embodies the love and goodness of the Creator. Standing in stark contrast to modern philosophical conceptions of nature, Wirzba's work is sure to inspire a wave of theological explorations in both the academy and the church."

—**C. Christopher Smith**, founding editor, *The Englewood Review of Books*; coauthor of *Slow Church*

THE CHURCH AND POSTMODERN CULTURE

James K. A. Smith, series editor
www.churchandpomo.org

The Church and Postmodern Culture series features high-profile theorists in continental philosophy and contemporary theology writing for a broad, nonspecialist audience interested in the impact of postmodern theory on the faith and practice of the church.

Also available in the series

James K. A. Smith, *Who's Afraid of Postmodernism? Taking Derrida, Lyotard, and Foucault to Church*

John D. Caputo, *What Would Jesus Deconstruct? The Good News of Postmodernism for the Church*

Carl Raschke, *GloboChrist: The Great Commission Takes a Postmodern Turn*

Graham Ward, *The Politics of Discipleship: Becoming Postmaterial Citizens*

Merold Westphal, *Whose Community? Which Interpretation? Philosophical Hermeneutics for the Church*

Daniel M. Bell Jr., *The Economy of Desire: Christianity and Capitalism in a Postmodern World*

Bruce Ellis Benson, *Liturgy as a Way of Life: Embodying the Arts in Christian Worship*

James K. A. Smith, *Who's Afraid of Relativism? Community, Contingency, and Creaturehood*

Christian Scharen, *Fieldwork in Theology: Exploring the Social Context of God's Work in the World*

From Nature to Creation

A Christian Vision for Understanding and Loving Our World

Norman Wirzba

B

Baker Academic

a division of Baker Publishing Group

Grand Rapids, Michigan

Published by Baker Academic
a division of Baker Publishing Group
P.O. Box 6287, Grand Rapids, MI 49516-6287
www.bakeracademic.com

Printed in the United States of America

Library of Congress Cataloging-in-Publication Data
Wirzba, Norman.
From nature to creation : a Christian vision for understanding and loving our world / Norman Wirzba.
pages cm — (The church and postmodern culture)
Includes index.
ISBN 978-0-8010-9593-1 (pbk.)
1. Creation—Biblical teaching. 2. Nature—Religious aspects—Christianity. 3. Ecotheology. 4. Human ecology—Religious aspects—Christianity. I. Title.
BS680.C69W565 2015
231.7′65—dc23 2015015876

15 16 17 18 19 20 21 7 6 5 4 3 2 1

For Bruce Ellis Benson,
John D. Caputo,
Adriaan Peperzak,
and Merold Westphal

Contents

Series Preface ix

Acknowledgments xi

Introduction 1

1. On Not Knowing Where or Who We Are 6
2. Idolizing Nature 31
3. Perceiving Creation 60
4. The Human Art of Creaturely Life 95
5. Giving Thanks 130

Index 159

Series Preface

Current discussions in the church—from emergent "postmodern" congregations to mainline "missional" congregations—are increasingly grappling with philosophical and theoretical questions related to postmodernity. In fact, it could be argued that developments in postmodern theory (especially questions of "post-foundationalist" epistemologies) have contributed to the breakdown of former barriers between evangelical, mainline, and Catholic faith communities. Postliberalism—a related "effect" of postmodernism—has engendered a new, confessional ecumenism wherein we find nondenominational evangelical congregations, mainline Protestant churches, and Catholic parishes all wrestling with the challenges of postmodernism and drawing on the culture of postmodernity as an opportunity for rethinking the shape of our churches.

This context presents an exciting opportunity for contemporary philosophy and critical theory to "hit the ground," so to speak, by allowing high-level work in postmodern theory to serve the church's practice—including all the kinds of congregations and communions noted above. The goal of this series is to bring together high-profile theorists in continental philosophy and contemporary theology to write for a broad, nonspecialist audience interested in the impact of postmodern theory on the faith and practice of the church. Each book in the series will, from different angles and with different questions, undertake to answer questions such as, What does postmodern theory have to say about the shape of the church? How should concrete, in-the-pew and on-the-ground religious practices be impacted by postmodernism? What should the church look like in postmodernity? What has Paris to do with Jerusalem?

The series is ecumenical not only with respect to its ecclesial destinations but also with respect to the facets of continental philosophy and theory that are represented. A wide variety of theoretical commitments will be included, ranging from deconstruction to Radical Orthodoxy, including voices from Badiou to Žižek and the usual suspects in between (Nietzsche, Heidegger, Levinas, Derrida, Foucault, Irigaray, Rorty, and others). Insofar as postmodernism occasions a retrieval of ancient sources, these contemporary sources will be brought into dialogue with Augustine, Irenaeus, Aquinas, and other resources. Drawing on the wisdom of established scholars in the field, the series will provide accessible introductions to postmodern thought with the specific aim of exploring its impact on ecclesial practice. The books are offered, one might say, as French lessons for the church.

Acknowledgments

It is a pleasure for me to acknowledge and thank the many people who have made this book possible. Colleagues and friends at various institutions invited me to give lectures that eventually made their way into the chapters here. Special thanks go to the Philosophy Department at Calvin College for their invitation to give the 2013 Jellema Lectures (these eventually became chapters 2 and 3), and to Duke Divinity School, Wake Forest University's School of Divinity, and Blessed Earth for hosting a 2013 conference on farming and faith (called "Summoned toward Wholeness") at which a much earlier version of chapter 5 was presented. A version of chapter 4 was first presented at the Society for Continental Philosophy and Theology's biannual meeting in 2012 and then published in *Pro Ecclesia* (22, no. 1 [Winter 2013]).

I also thank the staff at the Louisville Institute for awarding me a 2014 Sabbatical Grant for Researchers, and the Association of Theological Schools and the Henry Luce Foundation for naming me a 2014–2015 Henry Luce III Fellow. The Colossian Forum has also given this work a welcome scholarly forum in which the ideas of this book could be heard and honed. The combined generous financial support of these institutions has been an encouragement, and has given me the needed time to bring this project to completion. Special thanks go to my dean, Richard Hays, for granting me the leave time to focus and write.

Several friends discussed with me and/or read portions of this book in draft stages, making valuable suggestions for improvement: Fred Bahnson, Wendell Berry, Brian Curry, Ellen Davis, Celia Deane-Drummond, Joelle Hathaway, Stanley Hauerwas, Judith Heyhoe, Willie Jennings, Randy Maddox, Jamie Smith, Bron Taylor, Merold Westphal, Anna Wirzba, Emily Wirzba, and Gretchen Ziegenhals. I am especially grateful to Mari Jorstad for compiling the index of this book. Their multiple kindnesses are a testimony to the love of God, and their friendship is a daily reminder of why gratitude is the fundamental disposition of a faithful life. Thank you!

I have dedicated this book to four friends and mentors—Merold Westphal, Adriaan Peperzak, Jack Caputo, and Bruce Ellis Benson—who have been with me from the beginning as I have navigated the terrain of continental philosophy and Christian thought. It has been a joy to share this journey with such gifted and generous human beings.

Introduction

For too long too many Christians have thought that the point of faith is to prepare people to enter a heavenly realm "somewhere beyond the blue." The story goes something like this: Life here is hard, often painful, and sometimes miserable and brutalizing. Though we may experience various pleasures, we must never forget that they are ephemeral, and sometimes a temptation to focus on the wrong place. It is best to endure what we can, and put our hope in the day when we are finally freed from the trials, tragedies, and temptations of this world.

This way of characterizing Christian life is a theological disaster. Why? Because it rejects and violates the good and beautiful world that God made, the world that is the object of God's daily concern and delight. God's abiding covenant of faithfulness is with all people and with "every living creature of all flesh" (Gen. 9:15). God does not abandon this world or seek an escape from it. As the psalmist (104) sees it, God is continually present to it, blessing each creature into the goodness and beauty that it uniquely is. What God most wants is for us to learn to live more responsibly and more charitably wherever we are. The point of faith is not to help us escape this life. It is, rather, to lead us more deeply into the movements of love that nurture and heal and celebrate the gifts of God.

From Scripture's beginning to its end we find God as the one who constantly desires to live intimately with us here on earth. God is not aloof, disinterested, or far removed from this world. In Genesis we first discover God with knees and hands in the dirt, breathing into soil the breath of life that creates you and me, along with all the plants and animals and birds. God is a Gardener who loves soil and delights in fertility. In Deuteronomy we find God delivering the Israelites into a promised land that is never without God's attending care: "The eyes of the LORD your God are always on it, from the beginning of the year to the end of the year" (11:12). The land itself—the hills and valleys, the fields and vineyards, the streams and animals, and the villages and homes—is good. This is why the prophet Amos envisions God's restoration of life as people being securely "planted" by God in the land that has been given to them, able to enjoy the food and drink and conviviality it provides. It is why the prophet Isaiah speaks of the re-creation of Jerusalem by God as a place of joy and delight.

In the New Testament God's commitment to be "with us" and to fully share in the life of this world becomes most intimate in the flesh of Jesus of Nazareth. Jesus does not ever dismiss or disparage bodies, even though they can clearly be the source of suffering and pain. Instead he heals and feeds and exorcises and touches the bodies of others so that they can each live into the fullness of their potential. Through the body of Jesus, God is actively reconciling all things in heaven and all things on earth, inviting them to share in the divine life that God is (Col. 1:15–20). God does not abandon creatures to themselves. God sends the Holy Spirit "upon all flesh" (Acts 2:17) as a sign of the coming of the great day of the Lord in which all who call upon God's name will be saved. And then, in an astounding concluding scene, rather than people *ascending* to heaven to enjoy life with God forever, God *descends* to earth to live with us in a world that has been healed and made new. John recalls a voice saying, "See, the home of God is among mortals. He will dwell with them; they will be his peoples, and God himself will be with them" (Rev. 21:3). Imagine the look of surprise on the faces of Christians who have departed earth to be with God, only to discover that they are moving in the wrong direction. God is coming here!

What sort of world will God find? Will God find among people followers who, like generous and kind hosts, are proud to make God welcome in a home that has been carefully tended and prepared for a joyful life together?

The wide scope of planet Earth's degradation and destruction suggests that many people, Christians included, do not believe this world matters much. Though it may have been created long ago as a "garden of delight," which is what Eden literally means, it has long lost many of its paradisiacal qualities. Who wants to dwell in a toxic swamp, a dead zone, or an asphalt strip mall? As a result, we do not find much of this world to be a home or a garden worth cherishing or inviting God to dwell in.

How did this come to be? What sorts of capacities do we need to develop so that this world and this life can be seen in a way similar to how God sees it: as good and beautiful, and as worthy of being cherished and celebrated?

In this book I suggest that Christians can start by developing an *imagination* for the world as created, sustained, and daily loved by God. I stress the development of an imaginative capacity because it has become evident that more knowledge or information about the earth is not, by itself, going to be of sufficient help. Never before have we had as much scientific data and technological sophistication as we have now. But as long as what we know comes to us through the lenses of money, control, and convenience—which is exactly what happens when science becomes beholden to the interests and the funding of industry and business—knowledge will not be enough. The degradation and the destruction will simply continue.

My complaint is not with science as such or with the discoveries it has made and will continue to make. It is with the diminishment of our capacities to have humility before and sympathy for the things we desire to know. What the exploitation and the engineering of our world clearly show is a basic contempt and a fundamental ingratitude for the gifts that are in it. If people are going to learn to receive the world *as a gift*, and then learn to nurture and share it, they are also going to need to appreciate and affirm it as a miracle that is itself an expression of divine love. Put simply, as desirable as it may be to have information about the world, what we most need are capacities that will help us love the world.

My call to develop an imaginative capacity is not an invitation to fantasy or wishful thinking. It is, rather, an admission that we need to be honest about the limits and the shortsightedness of so much of our instrumentalized, utilitarian seeing, and that we need to develop the sympathetic capacity that encourages us to see things in their particularity, their wholeness, and their (often hidden) potential. Imagination is thus a call to greater honesty because our first and forever fundamental task is to become more attentive to and patient before the world in all its detail and interconnectedness—a task rendered extremely difficult, if not impossible, by the contrasting desire to use the world for self-glorifying ends.

In a penetrating defense of the sanctity of the world, Wendell Berry has observed that

> the human necessity is not just to know, but also to cherish and protect the things that are known, and to know the things that can only be known by cherishing. If we are to protect the world's multitude of places and creatures, then we must know them, not just conceptually but imaginatively as well. They must be pictured in the mind and in memory; they must be known with affection, "by heart," so that in seeing or remembering them the heart may be said to "sing," to make music peculiar to its recognition of each particular place or creature that it knows well. . . . To know imaginatively is to know intimately, particularly, precisely, gratefully, reverently, and with affection.[1]

To know imaginatively is to try to see the world with the love by which God sees and sustains the world. Appropriately trained by this love, we may yet learn to contribute to the healing and the beautification of the world, and so witness to God's desire to be with us, God's desire to have each creature share in heaven's earthly life.

The stress has to be on love because it is only God's love that creates the world, just as it is the discipline of love that enables us to move more deeply into the world so as to know it truly. John's first letter put the matter bluntly: "Whoever does not love does not know God, for God is love" (1 John 4:8). The Christian task is to learn, by patterning our lives on Jesus, to participate in the ways of divine love—shared intimacy being the most profound sign of genuine understanding—and thereby discover fellowship with God and with the world. From a Christian point

1. Wendell Berry, *Life Is a Miracle: An Essay against Modern Superstition* (Washington, DC: Counterpoint, 2000), 137–38.

of view, we cannot properly know or live in the world if we do not share in the divine love that brings it into being and that sustains and leads it into its perfection.

In the chapters that follow I argue that major trends within modern and postmodern culture—utilitarian and instrumental thinking, the encouragement of an idolatrous temperament, the insularity of urban and suburban forms of life, the development of anonymous and community-destroying economic forms, and a pervasive, even methodological, ingratitude—undermine the possibility of this love. Not surprisingly, this time is characterized by the felt absence of God and the systematic degradation of the world. The two phenomena are inextricably linked.

If we are to change course, we need to pursue the art of love and practice its disciplines. For Christians this happens by being discipled into the ways of Jesus's life, ways that nurture, heal, reconcile, and celebrate the gifts of God. Being "in Christ," people are made new into the creatures God has always desired them to be (2 Cor. 5:17). Discipleship makes possible an iconic way of perceiving the world, a form of perception in which others are received and engaged as material expressions of God's love. Encountered as the blessing of God that it is, each creature becomes an occasion for gratitude and an invitation to cherish and delight in a world that is wonderfully made.

1

On Not Knowing Where or Who We Are

> If there is no God, then nature is not a creation, lovingly crafted and endowed with purpose and value by its Creator. It can only be a cosmic accident, dead matter contingently propelled by blind force, ordered by efficient causality. In such a context, a moral subject, living his life in terms of value and purpose, would indeed be an anomaly, precariously rising above it in a moment of Promethean defiance only to sink again into the absurdity from which he rose. If God were dead, so would nature be—and humans could be no more than embattled strangers, doomed to defeat, as we have largely convinced ourselves we in fact are.
>
> Erazim Kohák, *The Embers and the Stars*

Friedrich Nietzsche's famous declaration of the "death of God" has never simply been about the murder and burial of a divine being. It has also been about the "death of a world" and, alongside that, the death of a whole field of meaning and human responsibility. If God the *Creator* is dead, then so too is the world, understood as *God's creation*. When the world ceases to signify as God's creation, humanity's place within it, indeed the very idea of the human being *as creature*, undergoes profound transformation.

As Nietzsche described it in his aphorism "The Madman," the definitive sign of the death of God is God's absence from the world. The murderers of God, the ones Nietzsche identifies as normal people simply going about their day-to-day business, did not don some special armor and then scale some heavenly height to attack God. They didn't have to. For God to die and be consigned to a tomb—or the graveyard next to the church—all they needed to do was live as if God were irrelevant, or as if God did not matter for the way they built communities, ran economies, practiced politics, and fueled their ambitions. In other words, for God to die, all that is necessary is for people to imagine and implement a world in which God is an unwelcome, unnecessary, or unimaginable hypothesis. They only need to install themselves as godlike beings who bring whatever order and significance the world might be claimed to have. Consider it death by apathy, or arrogance, or boredom.

The murder of God is no simple thing. When God disappears, the whole world and human involvement with it changes. If at one time Christians may have thought life and material things had their meaning and significance in God (because the Triune God was believed to be their creator, sustainer, and ultimate fulfillment), to live in a modern or postmodern world means that things are . . . well, we are not exactly sure. Are we and the things of this world genuinely valuable or meaningful if merely moments within a cosmic accident or perhaps pawns in a random game? Does anything have abiding significance? Does it even matter what we do? Weighed down by the misery and cruelty of so much "life," we may well side with Shakespeare's Macbeth and judge that "life's but a walking shadow, a poor player / that struts and frets his hour upon the stage / and then is heard no more: it is a tale / told by an idiot, full of sound and fury, / signifying nothing" (5.5). Nietzsche's madman does not mince words about the gravity of our predicament:

> What were we doing when we unchained this earth from its sun? Whither is it moving now? Whither are we moving? Away from all suns? Are we not plunging continually? Backward, sideward, forward, in all directions? Is there still any up or down? Are we not straying through an infinite nothing? Do we not feel the breath of empty space? Has it not become colder? Is not night continually closing in on us?[1]

How does a person move when totally lost, or when the markers that direct us to home, or to the good and the true, are gone? Does it even make sense to talk about a good home or a worthwhile destination?

It would be silly, of course, to think that Nietzsche's proclamation somehow brought about God's death. Nietzsche is simply observing—clearly with personal approval—the slow asphyxiation of God that is the result of changes in practical and theoretical life that would come to dominate modern and postmodern existence: scientific reductionism, the autonomous self, instrumental reasoning, unencumbered individualism, technophilia, and the dis-embedding of communities from life-giving habitats (to name a few). Nietzsche did not kill God. We, insofar as we are participants in certain strands of the project called modernity, did. But to proclaim the death of God does not mean that we have learned to see or appreciate the implications of what we are doing. This is why Nietzsche says the madman smashed his lantern to the ground, saying, "This deed [the murder of God] is still more distant from them than the distant stars—*and yet they have done it themselves*."[2]

It is cool to say God has been ditched—that way you can at least separate yourself from a sordid history of God's followers—but how many people are fully prepared to ditch nonarbitrary meaning too? This is why many are unable to give up the religious veneer of lasting values or universal reason or some other God-surrogate. Terry Eagleton puts it well when he observes,

> As long as God's shoes have been filled by Reason, art, culture, *Geist*, imagination, the nation, humanity, the state, the people,

1. Friedrich Nietzsche, *The Gay Science*, trans. Walter Kaufmann (New York: Vintage Books, 1974), 181.

2. Ibid., 182 (emphasis original).

> society, morality, or some other such specious surrogate, the Supreme Being is not quite dead. He may be mortally sick, but he has delegated his affairs to one envoy or another, part of whose task is to convince men and women that there is no cause for alarm, that business will be conducted as usual despite the absence of the proprietor, and that the acting director is perfectly capable of handling all inquiries.[3]

The flip side of this scenario is that the continued visible presence of church buildings does not guarantee the presence of God. Nor does it assure us that the people inside them will live in a God-glorifying manner. The forces of modern culture and economy can be so dominant in the daily spheres of life—in the ways we shop, eat, run businesses, vote at elections, teach our young, and seek employment—that people can attend worship on holy days and be practical atheists for the rest. People can profess a verbal piety and claim they seek a taste of God, all the while consuming a steady diet of self-glorifying cakes. Put another way, just as proclaimed atheists may find it hard to ditch the bad faith and hypocrisy at work in the modern substitutes for God that provide consolation, so too proclaimed believers may not appreciate the hypocrisy of a misplaced faith that has not learned to seriously scrutinize the idols of modernity that have taken God's place.

Complete follow-through on the death of God is a package deal that includes the death of the world and the death of humanity at the same time. What you have to give up is the idea that meaning or value can be located or secured by God, the world, or a human subject. Have we arrived at this point? Some would say that we have, in the advanced stages of consumer capitalism, because in this context people are basically passive, occupying a provisional, endlessly changeable identity (or style)

3. Terry Eagleton, *Culture and the Death of God* (New Haven: Yale University Press, 2014), 151. As Eagleton sees it, Nietzsche understood that genuine atheism is much more difficult than simply avoiding a church: "What Nietzsche recognizes is that you can get rid of God only if you also do away with innate meaning. The Almighty can survive tragedy, but not absurdity. As long as there appears to be some immanent sense to things, one can always inquire after the source from which it springs" (155). This is why he wonders if Nietzsche's *Übermensch* (a mini-creator of values) is not a perpetuation of the deity, though in a rather desperate, and perhaps pathetic, form.

that is subject to the fickle and feckless forces of this or that marketing campaign. Consumer capitalism, in other words, would be the practical realization of a genuine, postmodern atheism because it marks the time in which the world and human life are shorn of all depth and significance.[4]

On Becoming Lost

To know *how to live* presupposes that we know *who we are* and *where we are*. For example, to be dressed in an athletic uniform and in a gym means that I am going to play a game of some sort. What I am to do follows from where I understand myself to be located (an athletic facility) and who I perceive myself to be (an athlete). But what if it is impossible for me to know that the place I am in *is* a gym and that I *am* an athlete, which places and calls me into a particular kind of role? This is the situation the madman is describing: when the earth became unchained from the sun—that is, when the world lost its inspiration and orientation in God the Creator—then the markers or signs that identify the world (as creation) and us (as creatures called to particular affections and responsibilities) disappeared also. Without God as Creator it simply makes no sense to think of the world as a place of divinely cherished gifts or as a divine theater in which creatures are loved by God and we are invited to play a contributing role in a drama that seeks the full flourishing of all. We become, as Macbeth suspected, "poor players" who have lost the sense to know that something of eternal significance is going on. Given sufficient darkness, it is but a matter of time before we feel ourselves to be moving through an infinite, but empty, nothing. Given enough time in the darkness, people inevitably lose awareness of their own destructiveness. They lose the sense of what has been lost, or that anything could be lost at all.

4. "Given its pragmatic, utilitarian bent, capitalism, especially in its post-industrial incarnation, is an intrinsically faithless social order. Too much belief is neither necessary nor desirable for its operations. Beliefs are potentially contentious affairs, which is good neither for business nor for political stability. They are also commercially superfluous. . . . As long as its citizens roll into work, pay their taxes and refrain from assaulting police officers, they can believe pretty much what they like" (ibid., 195).

In a celebrated address entitled "Without God," Steven Weinberg, a Nobel Prize–winning physicist, said it is time for us to learn to live in a world that is dark and pointless. In making this suggestion Weinberg said he was not simply offering his opinion. The work of good inquiry and analysis requires that we come to this conclusion. The findings of modern science present us with a world that is without ultimate meaning and value. Weinberg admits that this is a "rather chilling" picture:

> Not only do we not find any point to life laid out for us in nature, no objective basis for our moral principles, no correspondence between what we think is the moral law and laws of nature, of the sort imagined by philosophers from Anaximander and Plato to Emerson. We even learn that the emotions that we most treasure, our love for our wives and husbands and children, are made possible by chemical processes in our brains that are what they are as the result of natural selection acting on chance mutations over millions of years.[5]

If it is indeed the case that random, chance occurrences account for the universe and for the ways we might learn to love any of it, then it is also clear that any demonstration of affection, any effort to think our world a valuable home, is a random fluke. Love is finally silly because it is but the effluence of random chemical perturbations.

An accidental universe can have no abiding significance or worth. It can evoke little devotion or lasting commitment to care for it. Though we might individually claim that some things and we ourselves matter, it is hard to know why anyone else should take such a claim seriously if it has been generated by a randomly produced mind and chemically fickle heart. You can admire your world, but I'll do with mine as I please! According to Weinberg, we will have finally become honest about the world and ourselves when we "get out of the habit of worshipping anything."

Weinberg's account is one in which disaffection and, practically speaking, destruction finally rule. Though he is proud

5. Steven Weinberg, "Without God," *New York Review of Books*, September 25, 2008, http://www.nybooks.com/articles/archives/2008/sep/25/without-god/.

of science's ability to determine and describe mathematically how the world works (but even here he is cautious, noting that "we will never get to the bottom of things, because whatever theory unifies all observed particles and forces, we will never know why it is that that theory describes the real world and not some other theory"), our situation is fundamentally one of disorientation. Whichever way we might orient ourselves is but the reflection of a groundless theory that is the product of a brain functioning in an accidental way. Or, more cynically and practically, the way we live is a feature of how much and what kind of power we happen to have at our disposal. In this world of pointless struggle it is impossible to distinguish destruction or devotion because the requirement of fidelity to and responsibility for things has been undermined.

In the wake of the death of God no existing thing expresses or is the bearer of meaning that is internal or intrinsic to itself. Whatever significance things are claimed to have is surface and ephemeral, the reflection of a temporary meaning we, for whatever reason, have given them. This is why it makes little sense to describe the human task as fidelity to or care for the goodness of things. Something is claimed to be valuable only because I or a marketer or some influential thought-leader says so. Each person's appearance in the world and every particular place people find themselves in are nothing more than a fluke. One person's enhancement of the world can just as well be another's diminishment, a result which, from the point of view of advanced capitalism, is a wonderful place to be because it celebrates the unceasing, unfettered buying and selling and wasting of everything. And so we live "on a knife-edge, between wishful thinking on the one hand and, on the other, despair."[6]

Weinberg's sojourn along a knife's edge is little different from Nietzsche's straying through an infinite nothing. When honestly pursued, both paths leave us *and* the world lifeless and cold. How could they not, since for both thinkers this world and our life are a dark accident? But when life is characterized this way, it is all but inevitable that human action in the world, especially in its more desperate moments, will become dark and

6. Ibid.

destructive too: we take our cues on how to live from where and who we think ourselves to be.

Nietzsche's plea for the affirmation of life notwithstanding, the last several centuries are a depressing witness to the degrading and violent effects of a dark and futile life: fresh water has been poisoned and wasted by industrial and agricultural production; soils have been eroded and pumped full of ever-more toxic pesticides and fossil-fuel-derived fertilizers; whole mountains and underground shale deposits have been detonated to gain cheaper and more efficient access to their coal seams and natural gas; forests have been cleared for their lumber and to make room for industrial production of various commodities; glaciers and icepacks are melting and oceans have been rising and becoming more acidic as a result of accumulating greenhouse gases in the atmosphere; plant and animal species are going extinct at alarming rates; whole communities of creatures are being displaced and degraded to make room for various "development" projects; whole groups and races of people have been relegated to the status of cheap, expendable, replaceable, migrant labor, or they are deemed to be an inconvenient presence that must simply be expunged; and everything is for sale. The devastation of today's world and the degradation of many of its communities are, perhaps, a contemporary instance of the ground "crying out" (Gen. 4:10) in witness to the sins of wayward human hearts.

To be wayward means that we don't know where we are or who we are. The effect of our confusion is a world that is slowly but systematically being murdered as we casually, or sometimes desperately, search for paths of happiness. In ways that Nietzsche could not have foreseen, the world is in fact plunging into a kind of exhausted, dead nothingness. The "death of God," the "death of creation," and the "death of the creature" go hand in hand. In their shared death we find the demise of a good and beautiful world, and a good and beautiful human life.

Moving into Modernity

Modernity can be described in multiple ways. In this book I will describe it as the time of the eclipse of creation. What I mean by this eclipse is that the world and the variety of things within it ceased to signify as members within a divine drama of creation, salvation, and consummation. In this new world, humans cease to be creatures of God made to share in the divine delight in the goodness and beauty of things. Instead, all things are reducible to amoral, material elements that can be manipulated to suit a variety of purposes chosen by us. Even human bodies, as the eighteenth-century French philosopher and physician Julien Offray de La Mettrie argued, are little more than self-maintaining machines of varying complexity: "The human body is a machine *which winds its own springs*."[7] Rather than being fertile soil warmed and animated by divine breath (Gen. 2), human beings (along with all other creatures) are here reduced to mundane matter in motion.

La Mettrie's position, though perhaps startling to many of his contemporaries, has become fairly commonplace today. Consider the diagnosis of contemporary medicine given by the physician and philosopher Jeffrey Bishop. In his book *The Anticipatory Corpse: Medicine, Power, and the Care of the Dying*, he describes how the metaphysical and epistemological frameworks of modern medicine presuppose a dead body that has no purpose other than to go on in its functioning as long as possible:

> Medicine's metaphysical stance, then, is a metaphysics of material and efficient causation, concerned with the empirical realm of matter, effects, and the rational working out of their causes for the purposes of finding ways to control the material of bodies. . . . For Western medicine, and perhaps for scientific and technological thinking, the important problem . . . is how

7. Julien Offray de La Mettrie, *Man a Machine*, http://bactra.org/LaMettrie/Machine/ (emphasis added). La Mettrie insists that the human soul is an effect of a material body exercising one of its many capacities:

> But since all the faculties of the soul depend to such a degree on the proper organization of the brain and of the whole body, that apparently they are but this organization itself, the soul is clearly an enlightened machine. . . .
>
> The soul is therefore but an empty word, of which no one has any idea, and which an enlightened man should only use to signify the part in us that thinks. Given the least principle of motion, animated bodies will have all that is necessary for moving, feeling, thinking, repenting, or in a word for conducting themselves in the physical realm, and in the moral realm which depends upon it.

> to manipulate the body or psyche in order to get the effects we desire. Bodies have no purpose or meaning in themselves, except insofar as we direct those bodies according to our desires.[8]

A root problem with modern medicine, according to Bishop's assessment, is that people have lost the ability to perceive, appreciate, and cherish human bodies as alive and as embedded within a bewildering array of life-nurturing and life-inspiring relationships. It is much easier to deal with a dead body because as dead it does not call into question the truth claims we make about it. Mirroring Plato's flight from (and disparagement of) the flux of material, embodied life, and his desire to escape into the permanence of invisible and eternal forms, today's doctors are being trained to bracket and ignore the messiness of the lives of patients who eat, work, and live in families and communities because these "external factors" unnecessarily complicate the neat analysis of individual bodies described as physiological machines. The questions "What is a body for?" and "How do we know if a life is well lived?" and "How is health a feature of an entire living community?" are rarely given the attention they deserve. The question that dominates is, "What (mechanical or pharmaceutical) technologies can we devise to maximally extend physiological functioning?"

> For medicine proper, a *telos* is replaced with a terminus, and the corpse is always anticipated. At the end of life, if the only thing keeping the body alive is the prior decision to intervene in a failing mechanism, there is no longer any sense of the integrity of the living body. Medicine gave birth to the life-at-all-costs mentality, if only by machines that administer fluid and nutrition or keep blood oxygenated and circulating.[9]

The modern transformation of the conception of humanity reflected in La Mettrie, and then fully realized in today's medicine, assumes that people are creators of worlds of their own imagining. No material body possesses sacred worth or sanctity. Every material body, even the human body, is susceptible to manipulation.

8. Jeffrey P. Bishop, *The Anticipatory Corpse: Medicine, Power, and the Care of the Dying* (Notre Dame, IN: University of Notre Dame Press, 2011), 20–21.
9. Ibid., 279–80.

Renaissance philosophers like Marsilio Ficino argued that human freedom had become godlike. Given the inventiveness of human beings and their development of technological power and skill, it was their destiny to take hold of and refashion the world. Though ancient Greek and Roman thinkers were often anthropocentric in their understanding of humanity's place in the world, placing humans highest among all creatures, modern thinkers took the new step of lifting human beings out of creation altogether so as to rule over it in ways they saw fit. "[Man] will not be satisfied with the empire of this world, if, having conquered this one, he learns that there remains another world which he has not yet subjugated. . . . Thus man wishes no superior and no equal and will not permit anything to be left out and excluded from his rule. This status belongs to God alone. Therefore he seeks a divine condition."[10] By seeking this divine condition, people, in effect, refused their creaturely condition and instead assumed the role of a god. Rather than being priests or servants of creation charged with respecting, receiving, and offering the world to God and to each other, human beings increasingly came to see themselves as engineers and technicians left to invent and preside over what would soon become a disintegrating world.

To be sure, numerous scientists and philosophers of modernity continued to invoke the name of God, but the god they referred to bears little resemblance to the Creator as proclaimed in Psalm 104, who sends forth the creative spirit/breath that daily renews the face of the ground, or the Triune God who is intimately and constantly present to the world as its sustaining, beautifying, and perfecting end. The god of deism is a divine being that jump-started the universe long ago and then left it to run according to its own "natural" laws. This god could not possibly be the God of Scripture, because it is a mostly absent god, making only brief appearances in the form of "supernatural" miracles. A deist god, along with the mechanical world that is its inevitable correlate, could not possibly inspire or support a genuinely creaturely life.

Modernity ushered in a new world because it gave us a new picture and narration by which to conceive it, a picture that

10. Marsilio Ficino, *Platonic Theology* 14.4, quoted in Richard Bauckham, "Dominion Interpreted—A Historical Account," in *Living with Other Creatures: Green Exegesis and Theology* (Waco: Baylor University Press, 2011), 46.

would be of revolutionary significance for the ways people understand themselves and their place.[11] Nowhere is this more apparent than in today's industrial agriculture.

Just as human bodies have come to be understood as corpses to be fixed and manipulated, so too have land, plants, animals, and agricultural workers come to be seen as objects of control. By being reduced to a container for nitrogen, potassium, and phosphorous (the main fertilizers used in agriculture), soil has ceased to be a complex living thing that, by absorbing death, is the wellspring of the earth's fertility and life. Plants, meanwhile, are little more than stems and structures to be genetically manipulated so that crop yields can maximally increase or pharmaceuticals be produced. And animals, they too have been reduced to meat- or dairy-producing machines. As such they can be genetically engineered to grow bigger and faster (a financial success) even if such growth has the effect of eventual physiological collapse (a biological catastrophe).[12] Agricultural workers, in instances barely distinguishable from slaves, are often little more than muscle power purchased at the lowest price possible, all so that consumers can have food at the cheapest price possible. In this system, even food ceases to be a living, complex thing. It is but a more or less complex pile of nutrients that ought to be able to be engineered to give the fuel we need with the least possible amount of hassle.[13]

11. In her classic study *The Death of Nature: Women, Ecology and the Scientific Revolution* (San Francisco: Harper, 1980), Carolyn Merchant says, "Because nature was now viewed as a system of dead, inert particles moved by external, rather than inherent forces, the mechanical framework itself could legitimate the manipulation of nature" (193). Merchant shows how a picture of the world (as mechanism) goes hand in hand with a picture of humans primed to behave in certain sorts of ways (as wielders of power over it). A world conceived as a telos-free machine is the perfect context for people to exercise whatever power they can find in whatever way they choose. Merchant continues: "As a conceptual framework, the mechanical order had associated with it a framework of values based on power, fully compatible with the directions taken by commercial capitalism" (ibid.). We could add, a framework of values fully compatible with the aims of colonialism and the possession of lands and human slaves.

12. This is why today's meat production could not endure without the aid of numerous steroids, growth hormones, antibiotics, and other pharmaceuticals. Under today's growth regimen, most of these animals could not survive much past the time when they attain slaughter weight.

13. In "The End of Food" (*New Yorker*, May 12, 2014), Lizzie Widdicombe describes the efforts of Rob Rhinehart to develop Soylent, a liquid concoction

Industrial agriculture presupposes a metaphysics and an epistemology—a philosophical narration—of the world as one vast, manipulable corpse. As Wes Jackson, founder of the Land Institute, once said to me, much of today's agricultural practice is like the ICU in hospitals: the soil is hammered to death by poisons, only to be kept alive by various technological and pharmaceutical life-support systems. What Bishop says of the dream of medicine applies equally well to the dream of an ever-higher-yielding agriculture:

> People become caught in the dream that medicine can sustain mechanical life indefinitely. A metaphysics of efficient causation and an epistemology of stasis always result in a kind of violence, for one merely has to exert a greater force over the dying body in order to keep its matter in motion. The cold ground of medicinal knowledge—the dead body—and the cold efficiency of the body as a machine return with a vengeance in the lives of patients sustained on the machines of the ICU. The automatic function of the machine resists death.[14]

The Grammar of a Christian World

We need to appreciate that how the world is named and narrated—whether as creation or as a corpse—is of the greatest theoretical and practical importance because *the way we name and narrate the world determines how we are going to live within it*. In other words, how we characterize what things "are," what philosophers call the "being" or ontology of things, also determines what we are going to do with them.

For example, if I hold before you a plant of some sort and then proceed to name it a "flower," this will evoke in you a whole series of associations, feelings, and expectations. You will likely want to behold it or come close enough to appreciate its fragrant presence. You may even want to protect it because you want to admire its beauty for as long as possible. But if I name this same plant a "weed," a very different set of responses

that assembles the essential nutrients human bodies need to keep moving. Food and farming are both perceived by Rhinehart to be daily burdens that we need to learn to engineer our way out of.

14. Bishop, *Anticipatory Corpse*, 97.

is likely to arise within you. Rather than wanting to behold and protect the plant, you will instead want to eradicate it because weeds connote an intrusive and unwelcome presence. Then again, imagine that I say the same plant is not a flower or a weed but really a "vegetable" in an early stage of development. Now you will want neither to behold nor to eradicate it because you know that with sufficient care this plant will grow into a tomato or pepper plant that yields succulent and nutritious fruit. Indeed, you may come to think of this plant as an indispensable member of your household economy because vegetables feed you and thus make your life possible and potentially a delectable experience.

This brief ontological exercise demonstrates that the naming and the narrating of our world is no trivial thing. To say that our world *is* "creation" rather than a "corpse," a "material mechanism," or a "natural resource" means that we need to see it and our involvement with it in a particular, God-honoring sort of way. It is not a material mechanism that runs according to its own laws. It is instead the material manifestation of God's love operating within it. It is not a pointless exercise of motion, "full of sound and fury, / signifying nothing," but a drama that witnesses to a divine, hospitable intention that invites our response and participation. Therefore, the practices and priorities of our economies, and the way we think about production and consumption, need to reflect this new appreciation of the world. To live in creation, in other words, means that we must understand ourselves as called to adopt particular kinds of expectations, affections, and responsibilities that are appropriate to a world so named. If the world isn't a value-free, amoral mechanism, then we cannot do with it whatever we want. But if it is, as the poet Gerard Manley Hopkins once wrote, "charged with the grandeur of God," then we had better learn to attend to "the dearest freshness deep down things," and welcome the Holy Ghost, who broods over it "with warm breast and with ah! bright wings."[15]

Early Christian communities understood this. Their encounter with Jesus of Nazareth was quite literally a *world*-changing and a *life*-changing event. To truly meet Jesus means that things

15. Gerard Manley Hopkins, "God's Grandeur," in *Poems and Prose of Gerard Manley Hopkins*, selected and with an introduction by W. H. Gardner (New York: Penguin, 1953), 27.

are never simply things to do with however we please. They are, instead, creatures, each enfolded within the ministry of Jesus's life, each of them part of a divine drama that stretches from beginning to end and includes everything in between. And so they said a most astounding thing about Jesus and this world: "He is the image of the invisible God, the firstborn of all creation; for in him all things in heaven and on earth were created, things visible and invisible, whether thrones or dominions or rulers or powers—all things have been created through him and for him. He himself is before all things, and in him all things hold together" (Col. 1:15–17). Jesus is not only the Savior of the world. He is also its Creator. All things in heaven and on earth are created *in* and *through* him. They exist *for* him. That means that everything exists only because it has a place in the divine love Jesus made incarnate in his ministries. To see the world in a Christian manner we therefore need the optic that Jesus is and provides. Whatever we might think about the order or structure of the world must now be understood in terms of Jesus, because it is *in* him that all things "hold together." The same goes for the purpose, or end, of things: all things must ultimately be reconciled to God, and this can happen because of the peace that flows from the blood of Jesus's cross (1:20). If this is the case, then creatures can fully be themselves only as they witness and contribute to the loving life that he makes possible. For Christians the world *is* creation, and to know what creation means we have to look to Jesus and to the history of God's revelation, which finds its climax in him. If this is true, that means that when Christians look carefully at the world, when they peer beyond the surface of things, what they should see is Jesus and his love moving through everything.

To appreciate what is going on here we need to think of creation not as a teaching about the mechanics of how the world began. Considered this way, creation is primarily about origins. As developed in Scripture, however, creation describes the *character* of the world, why it is the way that it is, what its significance is, and what it is ultimately for. "Creation" names the ongoing reality of human beings, animals, plants, land, and weather, all connected to each other and bound to God as their source, inspiration, and end. As such, the teaching of creation provides a moral and spiritual map that enables us to see the significance of things and then move faithfully through the world. When we confine creation to an originating event, we lose the sense of it as a dynamic place so cherished that God enters into covenant relationship with it (Gen. 9:8–17), so beautiful that God promises to renew it (Isa. 65:17–25), and so valuable that God takes up residence within it (John 1:14 and Rev. 21:1–4). Creation is not a vast lump of valueless matter. It *is* God's love made visible, fragrant, tactile, audible, and delectable. Because God's love is eternally hospitable and always fresh, creation will always have a place in God's life. Insofar as creatures are wounded and suffering, God is at work to prepare a place in which "mourning and crying and pain will be no more" (Rev. 21:4).

This point cannot be emphasized enough. Owing to the long histories of dualism and gnosticism, many within Christianity cannot see how God's love of bodies and the material world is all-encompassing and eternal. The teaching of the incarnation notwithstanding—and the teaching of the resurrection of the body and the teaching of Jesus's bodily ascension into life with God the Father—many theologians believe bodies to be something that must finally be overcome and left behind. The result has been a disaster for Christian traditions, because it has so often led to a private faith and an abstract love that has little purpose beyond the transport of individual disembodied souls to a distant heaven. In the forgetting of creation as God's love made material, the whole of theological inquiry—what we think about God's character, the nature of the church, the extent and meaning of salvation, and the end toward which all life is moving—has become distorted. It has resulted in Christians who do not see the destruction of the created world as a problem!

Christian theologians of the early church regularly linked creation with salvation, and salvation with the embodied, practical ministries of Jesus. As Paul Blowers has recently shown in his magisterial study of early Christian thinking about these themes, "creation and redemption were seamlessly intertwined," with both being integral parts of a continuing divine project that reached its climax in the life of Jesus Christ.[16] Every phase

16. Paul M. Blowers, *Drama of the Divine Economy: Creator and Creation in Early Christian Theology and Piety* (Oxford: Oxford University Press, 2012), 12.

of Jesus's life—his birth and baptism, the performance of his miracles, his institution of the Eucharist, and his cross, resurrection, and ascension—had cosmic significance pointing to a new world.

Athanasius, the great fourth-century bishop from Alexandria, put it this way: "For it was fitting that while 'through him' all things came into being at the beginning, 'in him' all things should be set right (cf. John 1:3; Eph. 1:10). For at the beginning they came into being 'through' him; but afterwards, all having fallen, the Word was made flesh, and put it on, in order that 'in him' all should be set right."[17] For Athanasius the incarnation of God in Jesus Christ is of decisive significance for the whole world, because in Jesus's fleshly body the sin-caused divide between Creator and creatures is healed. Though creatures, especially humans, had fallen away from the life God desires for them, God "became flesh" so that creatures could be shown the way into true life. The Creator became a human creature, took on a human body, so that the bodies of creation might be freed from death and made incorruptible. Athanasius insists there is no inconsistency between creation and salvation, because "the renewal of creation has been wrought by the Self-same Word Who made it in the beginning."[18] Creation, we might say, flows *from* Jesus at its beginning, flows *through* Jesus as it is healed, and flows *to* Jesus as it is fulfilled. Jesus is the pivot of the universe's movement and the key to its deep meaning and significance.

Because of Jesus, Christians came to see *where* they were and *who* they were in a new way. The world was God's creation, and they were creatures within it. But to be creatures meant that they now needed to *behave* in creaturely ways suitable to their new location and identity. Hostility of mind and the doing of evil deeds are no longer appropriate for a world that is on its way to

---

"If there is a prime pattern of mimesis in patristic interpretation of the biblical witness to Creator and creation, it is the consistent emulation of their virtually seamless integration of creation and salvation" (245).

17. Athanasius, *In illud: Omnia mihi tradita sunt*, Patrologia graeca 25:212C, trans. in *Nicene and Post-Nicene Fathers*, second series, 4:88, quoted in slightly modified form in Blowers, *Drama of the Divine Economy*, 225.

18. Athanasius, *On the Incarnation*, trans. a religious of CSMV (Crestwood, NY: St. Vladimir's Seminary Press, 1977), 26 (§1).

being reconciled with God (Col. 1:21–22). Christians must live a life steadfast in the faith and confident in the hope promised by the gospel good news that has been proclaimed "to every creature under heaven" (1:23). Just as Jesus redefined the world, he was also re-creating humanity so that each person could live in a way that contributed to creation's flourishing. As the apostle Paul put it succinctly in his second letter to the Corinthians, insofar as people are "in Christ" they are no longer themselves: they are a "new creation" (2 Cor. 5:17), and part of a world in which the old is passing away and everything is becoming new.

To think this way about Jesus requires that we give up the notion that in Jesus God was mounting a massive rescue operation to save humanity (or, more specifically, human souls) from a damnable world. Such a view is fundamentally gnostic in its orientation, and represents a heresy the church has had to name and resist from the beginning. The second-century saint Irenaeus gave one of the earliest and still one of the most powerful refutations of this gnostic view by arguing that in Jesus Christ creation is "recapitulated." Based on Ephesians 1:10, where Paul says that all things in heaven and on earth are "gather[ed] up" in Christ, "recapitulation" describes the far-reaching action of Jesus to enter fully into the life of humanity and all creation so as to heal and transform it from within. Jesus, in his fleshly body, (a) brings unity between Creator and creatures; (b) rectifies the disobedience, corruption, and alienation that keep us from God; (c) as the New Adam leads humans to their complete fulfillment and perfection in God; (d) inaugurates in his resurrection an utterly new life for the whole of creation; (e) reveals the life that God has wanted for the world from the beginning; and (f) shows us what it means to live as God intends. Put in its most general formulation, God became a human creature so that in Jesus God could show us how to better imagine and fully become creatures ourselves.

According to Irenaeus, Jesus can do all these things because he is the fulfillment of God's eternal will, purpose, and plan. The summary of Blowers is helpful because it shows the wide effect of this way of thinking:

> Christ, through his incarnation, cross, and resurrection, counters and overcomes the cosmic grip of sin and death; he reverses

> the downward spiral of evil; he recovers creation from the weakness and vulnerability of corporeal nature. He liberates humanity from bondage to the "elemental spirits of the universe" (Col. 2:20; Gal. 4:3, 9). . . . Christ reconciles, pacifies, and unites all things in heaven and on earth (Eph. 1:10b; Col. 1:20), things naturally differentiated but subsequently polarized and alienated because of creaturely rebellion.[19]

To become a follower of Jesus was not to wait for the time when souls could be freed from bodies and plucked into an ethereal heaven. It was instead to see oneself as invited and inspired to join with Christ in the healing of the whole world. The reconciliation of all things in heaven and on earth that the Christ-hymn in Colossians describes happens through the blood of Christ's cross, which means it happens through the self-offering life that Jesus demonstrated in his ministries of healing, feeding, exorcising, attending to, and touching others. Each time Christians eat in remembrance of Jesus, they are invited to receive him as nurture so that they in turn can become a source of nurture for the world.[20]

Though it may seem strange to say, Christians live in a different world than non-Christians. To be sure, all people reside and depend on planet Earth, but we don't all see the same things. We don't see meaning and significance or imagine potential and loss, sorrow and hope, in the same ways. Christians do not live in "nature" or a "natural environment"—at least not as modernity came to describe them—and then do various Christian things. To think that were possible would be like showing up at a funeral in a basketball uniform ready to play ball. Christians live in a world that has been redefined and renewed by Jesus, which means that the *who*, *where*, and *how* of human life have been altered. If the place we live is creation, then it is time for us to be the kinds of creatures that live in a creaturely way. *Where* we are matters for *who* we think we are, and thus also for *how* we think it appropriate to act.

19. Blowers, *Drama of the Divine Economy*, 230–31. The summary of themes in the teaching of recapitulation is on 88–89. Irenaeus develops his position in *Against Heresies*.

20. I develop this theme in my chapter "Eucharistic Table Manners" in *Food and Faith: A Theology of Eating* (New York: Cambridge University Press, 2011).

Despairing of the World

That so much of creation is being destroyed is a clear witness to the fact that Christians have often forfeited their creaturely identity. The indictment offered by Wendell Berry, though painful to read, is an honest assessment of a profound failure of Christian imagination:

> The complicity of Christian priests, preachers, and missionaries in the cultural destruction and the economic exploitation of the primary peoples of the Western Hemisphere, as of traditional cultures around the world, is notorious. Throughout the five hundred years since Columbus's first landfall in the Bahamas, the evangelist has walked beside the conqueror and the merchant, too often blandly assuming that their causes were the same. Christian organizations, to this day, remain largely indifferent to the rape and plunder of the world and its traditional cultures. It is hardly too much to say that most Christian organizations are as happily indifferent to the ecological, cultural, and religious implications of industrial economics as are most industrial organizations. The certified Christian seems just as likely as anyone else to join the military-industrial conspiracy to murder creation.[21]

It is a contradiction to profess belief in God the Creator and then live in ways that degrade and destroy God's creation. That Christians have for so long endured this contradiction is a sign that they have failed to see themselves as creatures called to imagine the world in a distinctly Christian way. Put most generally, they have accepted an industrial and consumerist naming and narration of the world as a massive pile of "resources" waiting to be exploited by us.

In his book *The Christian Imagination: Theology and the Origins of Race*, Willie Jennings demonstrates that at modernity's birth European Christians did not simply steal land and people. Something much more profound was going on: namely, a redescription and renarration of what the world is and what it means to be human. Europeans installed themselves as a

21. Wendell Berry, "Christianity and the Survival of Creation," in *The Art of the Commonplace: The Agrarian Essays of Wendell Berry*, ed. Norman Wirzba (Washington, DC: Counterpoint, 2002), 305–6.

compass on the world, a compass in which they acted as the "true north" upon which all else depended for its significance and worth. White bodies became the benchmark by which black and brown bodies were to be evaluated, and white ways of organizing society and work became the standard that legitimated the genocide of peoples and extermination of indigenous ways of life. European invaders did not look at these "new lands" and their peoples and see the love of Jesus at work in them. Instead they saw "a system of potentialities, a mass of undeveloped, underdeveloped, unused, underutilized, misunderstood, not fully understood potentialities. Everything—from peoples and their bodies to plants and animals, from the ground and the sky—was subject to change, subjects for change, subjected to change."[22]

The land discovered by these Europeans was not perceived as God's creation and as a gift to be gratefully received and nurtured and shared. Instead it appeared as so much virgin territory and raw material waiting to be turned into a possession that could then be modified to enrich its holders. It did not dawn on these Christian missionaries that the land and its people might have integrity that deserved respect or even sanctity that called for appropriate regard. They could not see natives and African slaves as children of God nor whole continents as the material manifestations of God's hospitable love, because to do so would have required them to be critical of the economic naming and narration of the world that legitimated European imperialism. Give a boy a hammer and the whole world becomes a nail. Teach a person to think that the point of life is to acquire, and everything becomes a commodity. Form a nation to expect unending expansion and economic growth, and every land becomes territory waiting to be exploited.

Jennings helps us see that the modern European Christian imagination was (and continues to be) diseased. It had become infected so that it could no longer engage the world and its peoples from within a framework of God's love for it. Instead, people and land mattered only insofar as they could satisfy objectives that were thoroughly defined by the needs and desires

22. Willie James Jennings, *The Christian Imagination: Theology and the Origins of Race* (New Haven: Yale University Press, 2010), 43.

of white European (male) bodies. Because Europeans had established themselves in the position of a god designating value and significance, things could not appear as God's creation. Equally important, these same people could not allow themselves to be re-created by Christ so that they could meet and engage others in the nurturing and reconciling ways that his life and the work of the Holy Spirit make possible. And so rather than appearing to indigenous peoples—indeed, to their lands and animals—as witnesses to and agents of the "good news" proclaimed "to every creature under heaven" (Col. 1:23), these Christians represented a cultural and ecological catastrophe: instead of health, they brought disease; instead of fellowship, fragmentation; instead of peace, war; instead of joy, misery; instead of sharing, hoarding; and instead of life, death. At the core of these catastrophes we find "an abiding mutilation of a Christian vision of creation and our own creatureliness."[23]

It is tempting to think that we have moved beyond the colonial imagination that produced so much misery, degradation, and death. Contemporary fascination with what has come to be called "eco-apocalypse," however, should lead us to think otherwise. In film and fiction we see portrayed a world that has gone into varying states of collapse. The causes of ecocatastrophe vary, ranging from nuclear winter to genetic mutation to climate change. Sometimes the cause remains unmentioned, suggesting that there are any number of plausible ways that our planet and the cultural worlds it supports can come to an end. Has genetic engineering gotten out of control or into the wrong hands, unleashing superpests, disease, and mutant organisms into our world? Has carbon accumulation in the atmosphere gotten so high that all the glaciers and ice fields have melted, resulting in massive coastal flooding? Has the planet gotten so hot that fires and water shortages have created mini war zones in which people fight for what's left? Or has the world simply been consumed to death so there is no available energy, no nutritious food, no clean water, no breathable air, and no safety? What is clear is that a growing number of people feel that human beings do not know how to live in ways that do not precipitate destruction and death. Our desires and plans

23. Ibid., 293.

to make life comfortable for ourselves seem to have the reverse effect of compounding misery and doom.

Consider the highly acclaimed and much-read novel *The Road*, written by Cormac McCarthy. In the novel an unnamed catastrophe has struck the world, leaving it dark, colorless, and mostly barren of life. A man and his son travel this desolate landscape, holding on to each other for whatever comfort they can muster, looking to survive. McCarthy describes a world that has been rendered brutal, ugly, uninviting, and uninspiring, a world reduced to the following "absolute truth": "The cold relentless circling of the intestate earth. Darkness implacable. . . . The crushing black vacuum of the universe . . . Borrowed time and borrowed world and borrowed eyes with which to sorrow it."[24] In a land "looted, ransacked, ravaged. Rifled of every crumb" (129), the man wonders what there is to do, and why there would be any reason for doing it.

The father awakens one morning. "He lay listening to the water drip in the woods. Bedrock, this. The cold and the silence. The ashes of the late world carried on the bleak and temporal winds to and fro in the void. Carried forth and scattered and carried forth again. Everything uncoupled from its shoring. Unsupported in the ashen air. Sustained by a breath, trembling and brief. If only my heart were stone" (11). He rises and looks to the gray sky. "Are you there? he whispered. Will I see you at the last? Have you a neck by which to throttle you? Have you a heart? Damn you eternally have you a soul? Oh God, he whispered. Oh God" (11–12). It is hard to know if the man is talking to himself or to some hoped-for God. How can one ask for the God of life in the face of so much devastation? Why even try to survive if you're "the walking dead in a horror film" (55)? An old man met on the road sees it fairly plainly: "Where men can't live gods fare no better" (172).

But the man and his son continue, trying to make their way to the coast. What becomes clear is that it is the man's love for his son that keeps him going and that gives him whatever glimmer of light he finds in the darkness. The child's life, and the father's need to protect and care for it, is the only thing that

24. Cormac McCarthy, *The Road* (New York: Vintage International, 2006), 130. Hereafter cited in text.

stands between the man and his own death. "He knew only that the child was his warrant. He said: If he is not the word of God God never spoke" (5). One evening while the father watches his son stoke a fire, the father observes "God's own firedrake. The sparks rushed upward and died in the starless dark. Not all dying words are true and this blessing is no less real for being shorn of its ground" (31). Darkness and desolation notwithstanding, we are left to wonder if it is a father's love for his son, or perhaps a human being's fidelity to any creature, that will make it possible for a word of blessing to be spoken.

McCarthy paints a world in which creation and its Creator are taken to be absent. At one point the man says, "There is no God and we are his prophets" (170). The world has become a more fragile place than anyone could have thought: "How much was gone already? The sacred idiom shorn of its referents and so of its reality. Drawing down like something trying to preserve heat. In time to wink out forever" (89). Though the man and the boy move, a sense of fear and desperation accompanies them on their way. Violence, scarcity, and desolation meet them at every turn. What they hold on to are the few moments when gratitude (for some found food) and kindness (the son and the father for each other) protect them from envying the dead. Love, it seems, is all that can hold them back from total oblivion. But the love the father shows is itself a fragile and terrifying reality, causing him to be brutalizing to another starving man met on the road. Can this father's love be trusted if it depends on a gun? Can the love of anyone survive in a desolate world? How do we know if the love we need to live is real or authentic?

McCarthy is no Christian apologist, and his novel *The Road* provides no easy answers to these questions. His work invites us to think carefully about the world we are in and to question the ways we have developed to name and narrate our place within it. Decades of war, the invention and application of millions of gallons of poison, the unparalleled extinction rate of plant and animal species, and the systemic degradation of all the world's ecosystems indicate that humanity is engaging in the wholesale murder of every living thing. Are we not like the man standing out on a concrete causeway looking out onto a dead world? "Perhaps in the world's destruction it would be possible at last to see how it was made. Oceans, mountains. The ponderous counterspectacle of things ceasing to be. The sweeping waste, hydroptic and coldly secular. The silence" (274).

In this book I suggest that Christians learn the art of creaturely life. By *creatureliness* I mean a human life that tries to be attuned to God as Creator and the world as God's creation, a life inspired and directed by the true and complete human creature Jesus Christ. I do not claim that a creaturely life will be easy, partly because we live in a world so beset by degradation, but also because many Christians have yet to think deeply about what a naming of the world as creation means and entails. Forms of thinking and practice have seized the modern Western imagination (and many of the Christians within it) in such a way as to render the world inhospitable to the divine love that first created and daily refreshes it. Viewed fundamentally, Christians, by forgetting the teaching of creation, no longer know where or who they are.

People all around sense the disaffection and disorientation that dominate our world. But the restlessness and boredom, as well as the fretfulness and fatigue, that define so much postmodern culture are not the last word. For Christians there is the hope revealed in the creating Word who became flesh in the person of Jesus Christ. "All things," says the Gospel of John, "came into being through him, and without him not one thing came into being. What has come into being in him was life, and the life was the light of all people. The light shines in the darkness, and the darkness did not overcome it" (John 1:3–5).

2

Idolizing Nature

> The idol must fix the distant and diffuse divinity and assure us of its presence, of its power, of its availability. Just as our experience precedes the face of the divine, so our vital interest proceeds from it: the idol fixes the divine for us permanently, for a commerce where the human hems in the divine from all angles.
>
> Jean-Luc Marion, *The Idol and Distance*

The idea of nature, particularly as it has developed in some of its forms, represents a serious obstacle to Christian ways of inhabiting the world. When we accept a narration of the world as nature—by treating it as a stockpile of "natural resources," for instance—we not only learn to see the world in a particular sort of way, but we also commit to practices and ways of living that have the effect of undermining God's intentions for the world and for us. How we name and narrate the world matters. We have seen this already by simply considering the question of naming a plant a weed versus calling it a flower or a vegetable. Weeds we try to eradicate, whereas flowers and vegetables we enjoy by beholding or eating.

According to Scripture, the world we live in is God's creation. It is the visual, fragrant, audible, touchable, and tastable manifestation of God's love, the place where God's desire that others *be* and *be well* finds earthly expression. Nature and creation are not the same. Each presupposes distinct logics or ways of making sense of the world. To be fair, the ideas of nature and creation have complex histories and diverse expressions, making it impossible to speak of a single logic for each. Moreover, these logics are not always in opposition to each other, though sometimes they clearly are. This is why it is so important to clarify how either term is being used. Neither "nature" nor "creation" is univocal in meaning or innocent in its intended use.

My proposal is not that nature is evil. Nor am I advocating that Christians stop all use of the term. Instead, I am asking that we think very carefully about how the word "nature" is being deployed in a given context, and then determine whether or not such a deployment resonates with a Christian understanding of the world. As writers like Timothy Morton have observed, the term "nature" has been put to so many (often contradictory) uses that it confuses far more than it clarifies the world. He is particularly vexed by "nature writers" who mistakenly, he believes, advocate for nature as some separable, stable, transcendent reality that can then be used as a standard to legitimate normative claims about how social relations and the material world should be ordered, and argues instead that such a reality has never existed.[1]

"Nature" is one of the most complex words in the English language.[2] It does not mean one thing. In its varied usage it is

1. See Timothy Morton, *Ecology without Nature: Rethinking Environmental Aesthetics* (Cambridge, MA: Harvard University Press, 2007). I do not go as far as Morton in suggesting that "we should *really* drop" (13) the term "nature" altogether. Giving up on nature, however, does not mean that we give up on the world. What Morton seeks are ways of living in the world that take seriously our entanglements within it. For a variety of historical reasons, "nature" has been made to act as a foil that gets in the way of human responsibility for living in the world. It has been set up as an object or realm of facts "out there," apart from culture and human inventiveness, and thus reinforces conceptions that reestablish the very separations from the world that nature writers are trying to overcome (135). Morton seeks to undermine "the naturalness of the stories we tell about how we are involved in nature" (187).

2. Raymond Williams, *Keywords: A Vocabulary of Culture and Society*, rev. ed. (New York: Oxford University Press, 1983), 219.

clear that sometimes the word is little more than a projection of how we want or wish the world to be: think about how some actions are routinely condemned because they are purported to be "unnatural." When nature is reduced to a realm in which people set the conditions for its meaning and use, a reduction that clearly happened in modernity and is still prevalent today, then the idea of nature can be said to be the outcome of an idolatrous vision (more of what that means later). What I want to show in this chapter is that an idolatrous conception of nature became especially pronounced in modern, industrial societies, and that this idea gave rise to an economy profoundly at odds with Christian ways of conceiving and living in the world. We will begin, however, with some historical background as a way of showing how nature can be understood in radically different ways.

Which Nature?

Among several, but by no means all, ancient philosophers, the Greek word *physis* (translated into English as "nature") referred to the principle whereby a thing is what it is or the powers and processes by which it achieves its end. According to this tradition, it is "in the nature of" a wheat seed to germinate and grow into a seed-bearing plant. Similarly, it is in the nature of a human being to mature into a thinking animal. Nature is the reason and power within things enabling them to be what they are.[3] Insofar as things do not achieve or are rendered incapable of fulfilling their end, they fail to exist according to their natures.

This view of nature had important ethical implications, because it suggested that people live well to the extent that they bring their reason into harmonious alignment with the natural (sometimes personified) reason at work in the world. Human

3. The enlivening power of nature (expressed with a verb) soon came to be personified as Nature (noun), a reason or force that, though showing itself in the movements of the world, was nonetheless concealed from direct human view. Think here of Heraclitus's well-known 123rd aphorism "Nature loves to hide." Modern science would set for itself as a primary goal the unveiling of the secrets of Nature so that they could be put in service of human aims. See Pierre Hadot, *The Veil of Isis: An Essay on the History of the Idea of Nature* (Cambridge, MA: Harvard University Press, 2006), 29–36.

order should overlap and work in concert with the natural order that gives us a world called a cosmos (in its Greek usage *kosmos* referred both to "the order of all things" and to "the totality of the world"). Numerous thinkers argued that nature's action in the world is best understood as the production of a work of art. Aristotle, for instance, argued that Nature is a wise artist that orders the world in a rational, fecund manner, and wastes nothing. As such, it exhibits proportion, symmetry, harmony, and cohesion. Human art, the creative means by which we live into the world, is good and beautiful when it is inspired by and flows within the art that nature is. The Stoics expressed this sensibility concisely in their admonition to "live according to Nature."[4]

It would be naïve to suppose that ancient views stressed only harmonious order between human and natural art. Precisely because nature refers to the power that moves the world, humans could set as their task the exploitation of this power to improve their lot in life. In other words, people could engage in the arts of *contemplation*, whereby they came to understand and live within the order that governed their lives, but also the arts of *utilization*, whereby they developed the techniques enabling them to harness and redirect the powers that animate the world. Symbolized by the figure of Prometheus, the latter sensibility put humanity on a path to the domination of nature.[5]

It is important to underscore that human domination of nature can take multiple forms, and that it does not necessarily or immediately imply ruthless exploitation. The quest for domination is ancient because it is born out of the perennial, practical realization that human life in the world is hard, and

4. Rémi Brague's *The Wisdom of the World: The Human Experience of the Universe in Western Thought* (Chicago: University of Chicago Press, 2003) gives a nuanced account of the diverse ways in which the world was understood to form a rational, cosmic whole that guides human action.

5. Hadot distinguishes these two paths in terms of the figures of Orpheus and Prometheus: "Whereas the Promethean attitude is inspired by audacity, boundless curiosity, the will to power, and the search for utility, the Orphic attitude, by contrast, is inspired by respect in the face of mystery and disinterestedness" (*Veil of Isis*, 96). In the modern period, as scientists like Francis Bacon and René Descartes made clear, the Promethean attitude would win out over the Orphic. Even so, the Orphic attitude never entirely disappeared, because one cannot "use" nature without also learning to understand, and in some sense "respect," it.

that sometimes nature's effects do not neatly align with human desires but produce pain and suffering instead. This is why the practice of "mechanics" was understood to be a kind of "trickery" whereby people developed the techniques enabling them to get the upper hand over nature. In Pierre Hadot's translation of the anonymous third-to-second-century-BCE Greek text *Problemata mechanica*, we read: "In many cases, nature produces effects that are contrary to our interests, for nature always acts in the same way, and simply, whereas what is useful to us often changes. Therefore, when an effect contrary to nature must be produced . . . the cooperation of *tekhnē* is required. This is why we call the part of *tekhnē* intended to help us in such difficulties 'trickery' [*mēkhanē*]."[6] People devoted themselves to the mechanical arts (but also magic) so that they could learn to manipulate the powers of nature to satisfy their desire for comfort and position. Consequently, machines would come to play such an important role in society because they enabled people to produce effects (like lifting enormous weights or diverting the flows of waters) that deviate from, or appear contrary to, the patterns and effects of nature.

This brief look at an ancient characterization of nature as the *power* at work within things reveals its striking contrast with the more recent view that nature means wilderness, the wild world outdoors, the world of objects and living things that exist independently of human invention. Trees, whales, and deer, but also mountains, streams, and dirt, are all manifestations of this nature because they do not rely on human culture for their success. Wilderness signifies as nature in its most pristine form. Nature and culture are separate realms, defined, in some circles, by their opposition to each other. At times, civilization is characterized by wilderness advocates as an invariably degrading or destructive presence within nature (which is why native peoples who may have lived in a region for hundreds of years first needed to be removed to make way for a wilderness preserve). Humanity's most important task, therefore, is to love unspoiled nature and protect it, because it is there that humanity is made whole and fully alive.

6. Quoted in *Veil of Isis*, 102.

John Muir, founder of the Sierra Club, and one of the most influential nature writers of all time, believed that all people are born with an impulse to bond with rather than exploit the wilderness of this world. Writing to his friend Jeanne Carr, Muir said, "I am hopelessly and forever a mountaineer. . . . Civilization and fever and all the morbidness that has been hooted at me has not dimmed my glacial eye, and I care to live only to entice people to look at Nature's loveliness. My own special self is nothing."[7] Nature is only ever a good and benevolent order. Believing the whole world to be a church, and the mountains its altars, Muir claimed that if people could be taught to love nature, they would also find themselves most alive and in the presence of God.

In the words of his biographer Donald Worster, Muir, along with several Romantic poets, gave expression to a view of nature as

> a source of liberation, a place offering freedom and equality, a necessity for full human development, and, above all, a world independent of people to be defended and respected, even revered. Going into wild country freed one from the repressive hand of authority. Social deference faded in wild places. Economic rank ceased to matter so much. Bags of money were not needed for survival—only one's wits and knowledge. Nature offered a home to the potential maverick, the rebellious child, the outlaw or runaway slave, the soldier who refused to fight, and, by the late nineteenth century, the woman who climbed mountains to show her strength and independence.[8]

Given this view of nature, what was most important to Muir was to encourage in people a natural piety that would enable them to connect with the wild, harmonious life going on all around. Until such connection happened, people could not fully feel the joy of being alive.

It is well known that Muir's vision for wilderness was and continues to be a fundamental inspiration behind much of America's environmental movement. It can even be argued that

7. Quoted in Donald Worster, *A Passion for Nature: The Life of John Muir* (New York: Oxford University Press, 2008), 181.

8. Ibid., 9.

without him the National Parks system in the United States would not have come to be. But how should we assess his view of wilderness as nature shorn of culture's invariably spoiling influence, particularly when we see today that a "wilderness experience" often comes packaged as a consumer product that is itself dependent on economic practices that Muir would have found repulsive?

In a widely read analysis of the American idea of wilderness, the environmental historian William Cronon argued that even though wilderness has been presented as a refuge from the corrupting influences of culture, it is in fact a "profoundly human creation."[9] Wilderness may seem to be the most natural of ideas—because it would be the purest expression of nature—but what we see when we dig a bit beneath the surface is the invention and projection of human longings and desires. Cronon does not mean that wilderness is only or purely a social construction. He wants us to appreciate that how wilderness is pictured and presented changes depending on the time period.

To see how this is so, contrast Muir's characterization of wild nature as sacred with the perceptions of many of his earlier American counterparts, who thought of the wilderness as a mysterious, often dangerous (sometimes satanic) realm that fascinates, but also has the potential to do us harm. Early American settlers believed that if people are to inhabit wild lands, nature must first be subdued or conquered into submission. Following John Locke's position that it is human labor applied to the improvement of private property that makes land valuable, many believed that nature apart from humanity is worth nothing until it has been conscripted for some human purpose.

As the history of New World settlement shows, there was nothing necessary or inevitable about this process. Indigenous people, in many instances, did not live in such fearful, aggressive, or hostile relationships with their lands. Indeed, for many native peoples the idea of wilderness as a place apart from culture would have been a foreign notion: no place was "wild" because

9. "The Trouble with Wilderness; or, Getting Back to the Wrong Nature," in *Uncommon Ground: Rethinking the Human Place in Nature*, ed. William Cronon (New York: W. W. Norton, 1995), 69.

each place could be home. The fact that European settlement resulted in such destructive alteration of landscapes, and the genocide of millions of native people (thought to be wild and savage by their conquerors), is an indication that these settlers operated with a conception of nature as the realm to be overcome.[10] Culture's success requires the eradication of wilderness and nature's defeat.

As Cronon shows, the ideas of nature as sacred temple or as the place of satanic temptation were not the only two manifestations of wilderness at work in American society. The nineteenth- and early-twentieth-century historian Frederick Jackson Turner developed the idea of wilderness in service of the national myth of the frontier. "As Turner described the process, easterners and European immigrants, in moving to the wild unsettled lands of the frontier, shed the trappings of civilization, rediscovered their primitive racial energies, reinvented direct democratic institutions, and thereby reinfused themselves with a vigor, an independence, and a creativity that were the source of American democracy and national character."[11] Going to the wilderness, and applying oneself there, mattered because it was the place where one learned to become an (individual, white, male) American.

To these narrations of wilderness more could be added: the place of rugged individualism and authenticity, the destination of elite tourists, a storehouse of scenic views, or a carefully managed park with patrols and signs marking appropriate behavior. According to Cronon, history shows that wilderness is an invented reality that reflects the very culture many of its devotees sought to escape.

> Ever since the nineteenth century, celebrating wilderness has been an activity mainly for well-to-do city folks. Country people generally know far too much about working the land to regard *un*worked land as their ideal. In contrast, elite urban tourists and wealthy sportsmen projected their leisure-time frontier

10. A classic exposition of the American encounter with wild nature can be found in Roderick Nash, *Wilderness and the American Mind*, 4th ed. (New Haven: Yale University Press, 2001). See also Max Oelschlaeger, *The Idea of Wilderness: From Prehistory to the Age of Ecology* (New Haven: Yale University Press, 1993).

11. Cronon, "Trouble with Wilderness," 76.

> fantasies onto the American landscape and so created wilderness in their own image. . . .
>
> . . . Only people whose relation to the land was already alienated could hold up wilderness as a model for human life in nature, for the romantic ideology of wilderness leaves precisely nowhere for human beings actually to make their living from the land.[12]

The paradox of the romantic view of wilderness is that it results in a view of nature in which people are welcome only as tourists and in which they cannot make a durable home. By sequestering nature to that realm apart from culture, people give themselves an excuse to be inattentive to and irresponsible with the urban/suburban areas in which they live and the farm fields from which they draw their daily sustenance.

Modernity's Turn

My brief history of just two (among several) conceptions of nature—as the power at work within things, and as the wild realm apart from culture or civilization—shows that nature's meaning is anything but obvious. The moment someone utters the word, one should ask, "Which 'nature' do you mean?" It is important to be clear about this, because how we see ourselves and how we think we should act in the world are features of *where* we understand ourselves to be. Should we most try to contemplate the order of the world and then attempt to live harmoniously within it, or should we seek to recover the wildness within ourselves by encountering the wilderness outside?

Most people do not have a rigorously developed picture or account of where they think they are. They have not spent time studying cosmology or ecology, nor have they committed themselves to a clearly thought-out metaphysics that establishes the meaning, order, and value of things. Even so, their actions reveal, whether intentionally or not, that they are committed to a conception of the world that is far-reaching in its implications.

For instance, to live in the world primarily as a consumer means that the world will come to be understood as one vast

12. Ibid., 78–79, 80.

store or warehouse of commodities available for purchase. What matters most is that the world be made available to us efficiently, conveniently, copiously, and above all, cheaply. But why think of the world as a store? Why think of nature as one vast pile of resources waiting to be mined, harvested, processed, and marketed as consumer products? Is this way of thinking, a way that is clearly presupposed by capitalist economics, not the effect of an idolatrous impulse?

The idea that nature is more or less synonymous with a storehouse of "natural resources" now dominates the way many people think about the world. We see this in politicians and economists, along with the millions of people who have their retirements invested in various stock exchanges, who have become advocates for a growth economy. That such an economy clearly presupposes that planet Earth be mined and harvested beyond what is materially sustainable does not matter, because the desire for growth of GDP is so dominant, even blinding.[13]

The roots to this way of thinking go deeply into a variety of places. In the section that follows I will show that changes in the way nature and humanity came to be understood in modernity were of crucial significance in this development. Key philosophical commitments within modernity established a view of nature that recast the world as the place in which human beings became the arbiters of the value of everything, and thus also the masters of how things would be used.

How this happened makes for a very complex story, the details of which I will not rehearse here. One of its key elements, however, included the development of nominalism in late medieval thought. According to nominalist teachers like John Duns Scotus and William of Ockham, our thinking about reality depends on concepts (the "names" we give to things) that are independent of the reality they represent. The ancient idea that

13. The conceptual tool of humanity's "ecological footprint," first developed by the Canadian geographer William Rees, measures the amount of land, water, energy, fiber, and so forth that a particular lifestyle requires. In 2007 it was estimated that if everyone in the world lived the lifestyle of advanced, consumer societies, we would need 1.5 planet Earths to satisfy consumer demand. In other words, too many people are consuming at rates that exceed the capacity of ecosystems to regenerate. Growing the economy by increasing consumption is thus clearly a fool's commitment.

knowledge is a form of intimacy requiring a knower in some way to become what he or she knows (it is instructive that the Latin term for "to understand" [*sapere*] also means to have a taste for something in one's mouth), or the idea that understanding follows from deep, often practical involvement with what one attempts to know (recall that in premodern cultures the knowledge of the craftsman was often held as paradigmatic), is here abandoned. Reality and the ideas we have about it are separate. Concepts are not grounded in reality but find their source in the cultural conventions of the day. Not surprisingly, this separation made room for the kinds of radical skepticism about knowledge that would be the major preoccupation of modern philosophy.

Nominalism is about much more than a technical quibble concerning the nature of knowledge. Behind these epistemological worries there is an understanding about God and the world that is crucial for us to grasp. Nominalism defended a view of God as utterly unrestricted and fundamentally inscrutable in his power. Louis Dupré has captured the significance of this development in the following:

> A God defined under the primary attribute of "incomprehensible power" (*puissance incompréhensible*) excludes any motive beyond the exercise of that power. If he creates, his creative act does not bestow upon his creatures the kind of intrinsic intelligibility a theory of participative analogy between Creator and creature would grant them. The voluntarist conception initiated by John Duns Scotus offered, once radically thought through by nominalist theologians, no apriori guarantee of any teleology. It defined nature in terms of submission to a system of invariable forces causally imposed at the beginning.[14]

Nominalist theology, by stressing God's inscrutable power, severed God from the world in a way fundamentally at odds with scriptural traditions that stressed God's nurturing presence in creation. God has no reason for creating the world that is available to us, nor is God's wisdom or *logos* manifest in things made. God's relationship to the world is reduced to efficient

14. Louis Dupré, *Passage to Modernity: An Essay on the Hermeneutics of Nature and Culture* (New Haven: Yale University Press, 1993), 88.

causality. Though God may have gotten it all going, we have no answer to the questions why and for what end or purpose. The world thus ceases to signify as a realm of creatures reflecting a Creator's intentions. It is but the effect of an inscrutable divine cause.[15] Now the crucial move: since we cannot look to God as the source of the world's meaning, the only place to turn is to ourselves as the ones who will assign to the world whatever intelligibility or purpose it has.

This philosophical and theological shift, while abstract in its formulation, has immense existential and practical significance. If the form of God's life is entirely unavailable to us, blocked by an inscrutable, all-powerful will, then the meaning of a world believed to depend on this God is also gone. Looking at the world, we can no longer expect to see in it a divine intention or concern sustaining it and creating the conditions for a harmonious and beautiful life. As Bruce Foltz puts it, creation loses its "face," loses its transcendent depth, because it has been reduced to pure matter. "An outside alone, pure exteriority, is only a surface. It is a plane, a superficies; it is sheer extension. . . . It is unrelenting superficiality, and it is all-inclusive superficiality: not merely surface, but triviality, a surd surface, just there and nothing more. Lacking an interior, the surface relinquishes no face; it cannot face us, but is merely present."[16] If *where* one is does not matter, because it is understood to be the space of material bodies in random movement and accidental arrangement, then *how* one lives where one is ceases to matter as well. The

15. Gottfried Leibniz, in his correspondence with Samuel Clarke, observed that there is no real difference between absolute will (the idea that God's power is unlimited and unrestrained in every way) and absolute chance (the idea that power can manifest itself in any direction). "Will without reason would be the Epicureans' chance" (quoted in Hadot, *Veil of Isis*, 135).

16. Bruce V. Foltz, "Nature's Other Side: The Demise of Nature and the Phenomenology of Givenness," in *Rethinking Nature: Essays in Environmental Philosophy*, ed. Bruce V. Foltz and Robert Frodeman (Bloomington: Indiana University Press, 2004), 331. On the same page Foltz quotes Marcel Gauchet (from *The Disenchantment of the World: A Political History of Religion*, trans. Oscar Burge [Princeton: Princeton University Press, 1997], 95) on the practical implications following from a surd surface: "Disentangling the visible from the invisible made it 'inhuman' in our minds, by reducing it to mere matter. At the same time, this made it appear capable of being wholly adapted to humans, malleable in every aspect and open to unlimited appropriation."

significance of a human life no longer emerges in *response* to a meaningful or value-laden world. This is the world of Macbeth, in which the stories we tell about life could just as well be stories told by idiots.

Modernity represents a decisive shift in world- and self-understanding because it is at this time that the world's intelligibility and value are increasingly seen to depend on a meaning-*bestowing* rather than meaning-*discovering* self. Sense and significance cannot be grounded in God because God is inscrutable. Whatever sense the world is thought to have must therefore come from us. René Descartes's philosophical program reflected this fundamentally new orientation: the foundation for knowledge of any kind, indeed the meaning of all things, is grounded in the thinking subject. When humanity is the source of the world's meaning and value, a momentous practical transformation occurs, because we at the same time "render ourselves the masters and possessors of nature."[17] Bereft of a divine intention, the world is now opened to whatever intention, desire, or expectation we bring to it. As we will see, it is precisely within this shift that we can observe an idolatrous imagination fully at work.

In his essay "Modern Science, Metaphysics, and Mathematics," Martin Heidegger captured well how this shift in understanding led to a new conception of science that had a mathematical way of engaging reality at its heart. "The *mathémata*, the mathematical, is that 'about' things which we already know. Therefore we do not first get it out of things, but, in a certain way, we bring it already with us. . . . We can count three things only if we already know 'three.'"[18] Of course, numbers have been used by people for a long time, but in Heidegger's view a mathematical mentality emerges in modernity that firmly entrenches human beings as the center through which meaning circulates. Before Descartes, things in the world were thought to be subjects bearing sacred significance and independent

17. René Descartes, *Discourse on the Method of Rightly Conducting the Reason*, trans. Elizabeth Haldane and G. R. T. Ross (Cambridge: Cambridge University Press, 1911), 119.

18. Martin Heidegger, "Modern Science, Metaphysics, and Mathematics," in *Basic Writings*, ed. David Farrell Krell, rev. and exp. ed. (San Francisco: Harper, 1993), 276.

worth,[19] but after Descartes things became objects that have meaning insofar as they relate to the *cogito*, the thinking subject who assigns meaning from out of itself. "With the *cogito-sum*, reason now becomes *explicitly* posited according to its own demand as the first ground of all knowledge and the guideline of the determination of the things."[20]

To see the practical difference it makes to approach the world in a mathematical way we can note the difference between a road and a path as described by Wendell Berry.

> The difference between a path and a road is not only the obvious one. A path is little more than a habit that comes with knowledge of a place. It is a sort of ritual of familiarity. As a form, it is a form of contact with a known landscape. It is not destructive. It is the perfect adaptation, through experience and familiarity, of movement to place; it obeys the natural contours; such obstacles as it meets it goes around. A road, on the other hand, even the most primitive road, embodies a resistance against the landscape. Its reason is not simply the necessity for movement, but haste. Its wish is to *avoid* contact with the landscape; it seeks so far as possible to go over the country, rather than through it; its aspiration, as we see clearly in the example of the modern freeways, is to be a bridge; its tendency is to translate place into space in order to traverse it with the least effort. It is destructive, seeking to remove or destroy all obstacles in its way.[21]

19. One of the most daring expressions of this idea of the sacred significance of things can be found in Johannes Scotus Eriugena, an early medieval Irish philosopher, who argued that in creating the world God engages in self-revelation *and* self-creation because creation opens places in which the dynamic trinitarian love of God finds ever-fresh expression. Dermot Moran puts it this way: "This self-creation is understood by Eriugena as a self-expression, a speaking of the Word (*clamor dei*) which, at the same timeless moment in the process, brings about the creation of all other things, since, according to Scripture, all things are contained in the Word" ("The Secret Folds of Nature: Eriugena's Expansive Concept of Nature," in *Reimagining Nature: Pre-modern and Postmodern Confluences of Ecosemiotics*, ed. Alfred Siewers [Lewisburg, PA: Bucknell University Press, 2013], 119). No thing is ever simply a thing. It is also and always the material manifestation of God's self-revealing presence in the world. In other words, every creature, while remaining a creature, is a theophany.

20. Heidegger, "Modern Science, Metaphysics, and Mathematics," 304.

21. Wendell Berry, "A Native Hill," in *The Art of the Commonplace: The Agrarian Essays of Wendell Berry*, ed. Norman Wirzba (Washington, DC: Counterpoint, 2002), 12.

A road exemplifies a mathematical mentality because it engages a place not by attending to or respecting its particular features, but by imposing upon it an abstract idea determined by line, angle, and extent. In a mathematical world the qualities of things, the elements that make them unique and worth cherishing, disappear in our haste to reduce everything to a quantity that fits within mathematical models we have devised. There is in this mathematical reduction considerable hubris, because human ambition is taken to be the only concern that really matters. As the unparalleled alteration of our lands shows, there is also considerable violence.

Modernity, as we can now see, reflects a new understanding of human subjectivity. Numerous historians have shown that, starting in the twelfth and thirteenth centuries, a new type of individual emerges, a person who stands over and against the world as one who has the power to fundamentally transform it. If the purpose of a human life had at one time been to contemplate the world so that one could more harmoniously belong within it—hence the meaning of the personal noun "subject" as one "subject to" orders and purposes beyond one's own devising—now the purpose of life was to give expression *to oneself* in one's actions in the world. The name for this type of subject was the "architect" or the "engineer."

Along with the idea of the engineer came a new understanding of knowledge and science: knowledge is about the utilization of the world for human benefit and glorification rather than about its contemplation for the purposes of wonder and gratitude. Subjects are the masters and conquerors of a world now increasingly understood to be a mechanism. But as Dupré has rightly observed, this would turn out to be a lonely mastery. "In becoming pure project, the modern self has become severed from those sources [particularly God and nature] that once provided its content. The metaphysics of the ego isolates the self. It narrows selfhood to individual solitude and reduces the other to the status of object."[22]

So far we have seen that late medieval and modern thought put in motion a fundamentally new way of thinking about the self and its world. The world is simply matter in motion that

22. Dupré, *Passage to Modernity*, 119.

depends upon us for its significance or value. The self, rather than understanding itself as participating in and responsible to an order given with the world, stands above the world so as to impose an order upon it. To be sure, early modern scientists believed that as a natural mechanism the world had natural laws we must work hard to understand. But the purpose of understanding was increasingly to manipulate and dominate the world to satisfy objectives set by us. Carolyn Merchant describes the new "man of science" as an inquisitor: "Nature must be 'bound into service' and made a 'slave,' put 'in constraint' and 'molded' by the mechanical arts. The 'searchers and spies of nature' are to discover her plots and secrets."[23] Through scientific knowledge and technological innovation, people would aggressively remake the world so that it was more suited to human flourishing and comfort.

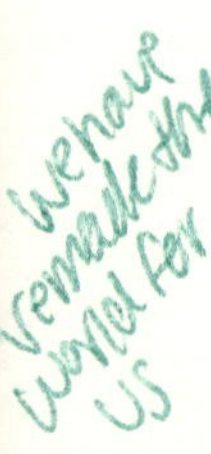

As we move further into the twenty-first century, it is plain that our innovation has been widely applied. We are remaking and reengineering the world in our image and to suit our desires at all levels, ranging from our alteration of the atmosphere's chemical composition (ozone depletion and greenhouse gas production) to the obliteration of mountains (to get to their coal more cheaply and efficiently) to the redesigning of plant and animal life's genetic codes. In this effort we are fulfilling the dream of the sixteenth-century visionary Giordano Bruno, who said,

> The gods have given man intelligence and hands, and have made him in their image, endowing him with a capacity superior to other animals. This capacity consists not only in the power to work in accordance with nature and the usual course of things, but beyond that and outside her laws, to the end that by fashioning, or having the power to fashion, other natures, other courses, other orders by means of his intelligence, with that freedom without which his resemblance to the deity would not exist, he might in the end make himself god of the earth.[24]

23. Carolyn Merchant, *The Death of Nature: Women, Ecology and the Scientific Revolution* (San Francisco: Harper, 1980), 169. For Merchant, the fact that these early scientists were men probing and exploiting a feminized Mother Nature is of vital significance because it testifies to a history of gender exploitation.

24. Giordano Bruno, *Spacio de la bestia trionfante* [The expulsion of the triumphant beast], quoted in Richard Bauckham's "Modern Domination of Nature—Historical Origins and Biblical Critique," in *Environmental Stewardship:*

What Bruno is describing is the prospect of human inventiveness no longer bound to a world as given. Freedom and intelligence equip us to invent new worlds, worlds that bear the imprint of human ambition and desire. Modern technological practice, rather than being inspired and informed by the natural or divine reason at work in the world, becomes the manifestation of a self *expressing itself* in the world.

What makes these modern developments unique, and especially important for our purposes, is not only that they characterized humanity as a conquering/mastering presence, but that they cast God as an unwelcome—really unnecessary—power. The modern scientific and technological mind, the mind-set that most dominates our world today, presupposes that nature is an autonomous realm that operates according to natural laws that we can understand and manipulate to our own ends. Nature does not find its sustenance, meaning, or end in God. Though God may have designed, even kick-started the universe, God remains external and irrelevant to it.

The idea that nature is a self-standing or autonomous realm, a material mechanism or random biological process that has no life or purpose in God, has profound cultural and economic implications. Dupré has rightly observed that this modern development introduced "a totally new way of confronting the real."

> The divine became relegated to a supernatural sphere separate from nature, with which it retained no more than [a] causal, external link. This removal of transcendence fundamentally affected the conveyance of meaning. Whereas previously meaning had been established in the very act of creation by a wise God, it now fell upon the human mind to interpret a cosmos, the structure of which had ceased to be given as intelligible. Instead of being an integral part of the cosmos, the person became the source of its meaning.[25]

Critical Perspectives—Past and Present, ed. R. J. Berry (London: T&T Clark, 2006), 36. Merchant quotes Francis Bacon (*The New Atlantis*), who also affirms that the task of humanity is not simply to respect existing organisms but to create new ones. Speaking as a forerunner of today's biotechnology advocates, Bacon notes that we "make [the trees and flowers of orchards and gardens] by art greater much than their nature, and their fruit greater and sweeter and of differing taste, smell, color, and figure, from their nature" (*Death of Nature*, 184).

25. Dupré, *Passage to Modernity*, 3 (the quotation "a totally new way of confronting the real" appears on 7).

To live in modernity, and to accept its naming and narration of the world as nature, is to commit to particular ways of seeing, understanding, and engaging reality. These ways are at odds with Christian ways. A helpful characterization of the difference is to say that the modern idea of nature is born out of an idolatrous impulse.

Making Sense of Idolatry

The central impulse in idolatry is not the worship of things but the worship of ourselves. Understood this way, idolatry is hardly a problem unique to modernity. People have long had to struggle with the temptation to glorify themselves at the expense of others and God. As the story of the fall of humanity in Genesis 3 suggests, we have had to learn to resist the desire to become little gods ourselves. Serpents abound, not just in gardens, tempting us with the idea that there are no limits to what we are permitted to do. The longing to know as God knows, and the hope that we will not suffer or die, are powerful urges that manifest themselves in all sorts of (often unrecognized) ways.

In the Ten Commandments the prohibition against idolatry follows after the proclamation that it was the Lord God who brought the Israelites out of the land of Egypt, rescuing them from a life of slavery. The God of Israel has liberating and thus trustworthy power, the sort of power that gives and sustains life. No other gods should be given allegiance, because they lack the power that leads people into life's freedom and promise (Egyptian gods, the Israelites should have remembered, sanctioned the oppression and abuse of life). Nor does any particular thing, whether in heaven, on earth, or in the water, have the power to bestow life. This is why the Israelites are instructed not to make idols of things (Exod. 20:4). Whenever we make an idol of any*thing*, we presuppose that it has the power to give life. We confuse something given by God as a *means* of life with its being the *source* and *fulfillment* of life. False worship is so dangerous because it witnesses to human attention and energy being directed in ways that are bound to lead to mutual harm.

It is customary to think that the prohibition against idolatry serves primarily to safeguard God's unique status as the only god worthy of worship, especially as Scripture recounts, "I the LORD your God am a jealous God" (Exod. 20:5). What we overlook, however, is that the prohibition also protects creatures. An idolatrous impulse compels us to place expectations on things that they simply cannot bear. We place our hope in something like personal wealth, believing that the more we have, the more secure and happy we will be. But property, possessions, and money cannot meet the heavy expectations we place upon them. They cannot save us. When we think they can we invariably get frustrated, demand more and better, and thus do damage to God's gifts and to ourselves. How many families, communities, ecosystems have been neglected, diminished, or destroyed by the pursuit of money?

Idols evoke worship in us because we think they can save us from life's contingencies, mysteries, and finitude. Put another way, we make idols of all sorts of things—the stock market, a job, superstar athletes and performers, our families—because we think that by giving our allegiance to them we will make our lives secure and complete. Viewed pragmatically, of course, stock markets can increase our monetary wealth, jobs can give meaning and shape to our daily schedules, superstars can give us a diversion or a thrill, and families can provide us with a sense of belonging and support. But none of these things in and of themselves have the power to give us or hold us within life. Stock markets crash, jobs are outsourced, superstars fade away, and family members eventually disappoint or depart. This does not make them evil. Received properly, they are each gifts given by God to enhance life.

But when we pin unrealistic hopes on them, forgetting that it is God alone who provides and sustains us all, we turn a gift into a god. We confuse where the power of life and life's true fulfillment ultimately reside. It is crucial to appreciate that this confusion prompts us to violate the integrity of others because we now make them serve personal insecurities and idolatrous fantasies. Prevented from fulfilling their own potential, they become frustrated, subject to futility and bondage, as the apostle Paul put it (Rom. 8:20–22). Ultimately, our confusion leads to the distortion of power and the destruction of life. It leads to the degradation of whatever we make into a god.

God's commandment against idolatry is God's way of saying, "Receive creation as a gift from me. Do not make the gift something it is not—a private possession, the object of your fancy, or the hope of your salvation—for when you do, you will destroy it and bring harm to yourselves. You will forget me as the one who cares for your every need. In your anxious desire to secure the world for yourself, you will do terrible things."

Whenever we think about idolatry, it is important to remember that idols are *made* by us. This means we have to pay particular attention to the kind of subjectivity that is prone to idolatry. What is it about us that prompts us to make idols?

In a series of penetrating reflections, Jean-Luc Marion has shown that idolatry is intimately tied to our desire to know the world. If we turn to Plato, one of the first philosophers to make the pursuit of knowledge an essential human task, we learn that the Greek word *eidōlon*, from which the English word "idol" is derived, refers to "that which is seen." Everything has an appearance or "form" that enables us to represent it and know it as the particular thing that it is. How we represent things matters greatly because it is through representations that we perceive, name, and engage whatever it is we claim to know. Knowing the form of a thing—is it a flower, a weed, a vegetable?—equips us to make sense of it by placing it within an ordered whole. It enables us to use it in various ways.

Practically speaking, there is a lot at stake in how things are named and ordered. Francis Bacon's claim that "knowledge is power," though written at the dawn of the seventeenth century, reflects a truth that has been operative throughout the history of humanity's attempts to know anything: what we know, and how we claim to know it, puts in place systems of order and frameworks of meaning and action that reflect structures of power. To "know," for instance, that women are not fully human because they lack a particular sort of rational capacity (Aristotle) means that women will be treated in ways deemed appropriate to their rank. To "know" that animals are complex machines or automatons (Descartes) means that vivisection can be performed without worry.

Though we live in a given world, an account of the world's meaning is not given alongside it. The world's significance, in other words, is something we have to discover and learn. It is something we have to work toward. How, then, do we come to have the representations and make the knowledge claims that we do? Marion insists that our looking at things is never innocent. Put too simply, people often see what they want to see. "The gaze makes the idol, not the idol the gaze—which means that the idol with its visibility fills the intention of the gaze, which wants nothing other than to see. The gaze precedes the idol because an aim precedes and gives rise to that at which it aims."[26] Our looking at something—how we look at it, and the fact that we are looking at it rather than something else—presupposes an interest and an intention. As people who *want to know* what something is, we have expectations, desires, and fears that invariably shape how something appears to us. This means that our looking at something is also at the same time (though not always knowingly) a looking at ourselves, because whatever we see is mediated by the boredom, anxiety, or hope we happen to feel. Our gazing at something includes a mirror reflection of the gazer's capacities, dispositions, and expectations.

Numerous examples can be given showing that the capacities, dispositions, and expectations in-forming our knowing can change. For instance, owing to considerable marketing and socialization, we have been trained to think about lawns as uniformly green carpets. The appearance of any plant other than bluegrass or fescue is automatically a weed because we expect "lawns" to look a certain sort of way. But why should we have this expectation? One might study soils and discover that a vibrant landscape includes a diversity of plants growing together. One might inquire into the health effects that follow from the steady application of poisons to eradicate so-called weeds and conclude that these effects are unacceptable. Or we might simply look more carefully at "weeds" like clover and dandelion and discover that they are beautiful, perhaps even nutritious. In other words, how we "see" a lawn changes

26. Jean-Luc Marion, *God without Being*, trans. Thomas A. Carlson (Chicago: University of Chicago Press, 1991), 10–11. See also Marion's earlier *The Idol and Distance: Five Studies*, trans. Thomas A. Carlson (New York: Fordham University Press, 2001), for a discussion of how idolatry functions in modern forms of philosophy. Bruce Ellis Benson has given a lucid treatment of the various forms of conceptual idolatry in *Graven Ideologies: Nietzsche, Derrida and Marion on Modern Idolatry* (Downers Grove, IL: InterVarsity, 2002).

depending on the (often marketing- or advertising-induced) sensibilities that the one doing the seeing has.

Marion stands in a stream of thinkers, ranging from Gregory of Nyssa and Pseudo-Dionysius to Friedrich Nietzsche and Emmanuel Levinas, who argue that we do not well enough appreciate how our seeing is an imposition of ourselves upon what is seen. We tend to think that our representations of others are "objective" and that our knowledge is disinterested, when in reality our thinking is always mediated through varying kinds of study and concern, even by something as basic as professional protocols and sources of funding for research.[27] Too often we fail to understand how power and desire function in the processes of knowing. Following Michel Foucault, we should acknowledge that our histories contain "regimes of truth" in which struggles are constantly being waged over which discourses are approved or legitimate, which mechanisms are used for distinguishing truth and falsity, which techniques for the acquisition of truth are deemed acceptable, and which persons or institutions shall act as arbiters and judges in the struggle.[28]

To appreciate that objectivity is a highly contested phenomenon does not mean that reality is nothing more than a social construction, a fleeting figment of our imaginations. What needs challenging is the idea that there is some underlying, inviolable reality called nature that does not change (the natural sciences are claimed to study this), while our awareness and

27. Bruno Latour argues in *The Politics of Nature* (Cambridge, MA: Harvard University Press, 2004) that our thinking about nature is always bound up with our attempts to know and use it. We operate within diverse scientific disciplines, using different tools and instruments, and within various professions and their databases, each of which yields its own "form" and interpretation of the world. Different time periods and their unique cultures embody different psychologies and thus different questions. In *An Inquiry into Modes of Existence: An Anthropology of the Moderns* (Cambridge, MA: Harvard University Press, 2013), Latour shows that the domain of science, taken by many to be an objective pursuit, is, in its practical working, entangled with the domains of economics, law, politics, religion, etc.

28. Michel Foucault, "Truth and Power," in *Power/Knowledge: Selected Interviews and Other Writings, 1972–1977*, ed. Colin Gordon (New York: Pantheon Books, 1980). Foucault notes that it would be impossible to emancipate truth from power because truth *is* power. His aim is to detach "the power of truth from the forms of hegemony, social, economic and cultural, within which it operates at the present [capitalist] time" (133).

cultural sensibilities do (the social sciences and humanities are claimed to study this). There is no "raw" access to the world, because the moment we try to enter the "objective world," we find ourselves already there. What we face is always a joint history of the human sciences and the physical world together. Bruno Latour wisely suggests that when we abandon the notion of a stable, unchanging nature, "we are leaving intact the two elements that matter the most to us: the multiplicity of non-humans and the enigma of their interaction [with us]."[29] We open a space in which genuine interaction and reciprocal learning between creatures can occur. We look for opportunities in which the reality of life together can inspire, correct, and inform our understanding.[30]

If the analyses I have provided so far are correct, then the histories of philosophy and religion can be interpreted as battles with idolatry and battles among competing idolatries. They are battles *with* idolatry insofar as we try to minimize the imposition of self-serving agendas and expectations on the world and God. They are battles *among* idolatries insofar as we imperiously claim to know fully the truth of what we seek, and thus feel authorized to compel others to see and order the world the same way we do. The challenge of thought is always to learn to be faithful to the world and honest about the claims we make about it. It is to be vigilant about the many forms of our inattention and mindful of the ignorance that permeates even our best efforts to understand.

More radical interpretations of our histories, such as the one offered by Levinas, suggest that the philosophical gesture is at its core a violent, totalizing gesture that reduces the integrity of others to the level of what we want or expect. In this idolatrous move there is no room for transcendence, and no opening for

29. Latour, *Politics of Nature*, 41. When we give up on the idea that culture works on nature "from the outside," we also liberate politics to become "the progressive composition of a common [human and extra-human] world to share" (47).

30. In *Environmental Culture: The Ecological Crisis of Reason* (London: Routledge, 2002), ecofeminist philosopher Val Plumwood argues for a nonanthropocentric democratic process that invites nonhuman creatures—their interests, potential, and significance—to the deliberative table. When people practically commit to be in solidarity with other creatures, the possibility exists for us "to create a new sense of the meaning of human lives by putting them into the larger contexts of the universe" (223).

the sanctity of others to shine through. Universal thought and action take the forms of "I think" and "I can," forms that secure the subject as the arbiter of reality and value. To "know" is to reduce otherness to the level of "the same," the level at which all reality is made to conform to horizons of meaning over which we have control.[31]

Even if one grants that much of our thinking tends toward idolatry, and that all too often we deny the radical otherness or alterity of others, this does not mean that thought and action are necessarily doomed to the confines of the gaze or the limits of a meaning horizon. We can identify and cultivate what Levinas calls a "metaphysical desire" that sees in another's being a form (*eidōlon*) or meaning that is not reducible to our expectations, hopes, or fears. This is an *ek*-static desire because it takes us *outside* of ourselves, opening us to the alterity and sanctity of whatever we meet. Rather than being an extension or fulfillment of our want and need, the form of another has the power to interrupt, inspire, and in-form me so that my inhabiting the world does not amount to a violation of it.[32]

We will return to what this faithful, ecstatic, response-able form of life looks like when we consider the meaning of creaturely life. But for now we can see that idolatry, understood as the imposition of the self upon the world for the purpose of the self's comfort, control, or glorification, is the temptation we must continually guard against. Idolatry is one of humanity's great sins because it encourages us to see and represent reality as, and thus limit reality to, the sphere of human power and convenience. It prompts us to reduce the world and God to the level of human appetite and expectation. Living in an idolatrous posture, we lose both God and the world.

31. Emmanuel Levinas, *Totality and Infinity: An Essay on Exteriority*, trans. Alphonso Lingis (Pittsburgh: Duquesne University Press, 1969), esp. sec. A. For Levinas, ontology—the science through which things come to be the things that they are—is a form of unjust power because it reduces otherness to sameness. It gives rise to the following definition of freedom: "to maintain oneself against the other despite every relation with the other to ensure the autarchy of an I" (46).

32. In *Otherwise Than Being, or Beyond Essence*, trans. Alphonso Lingis (The Hague: Martinus Nijhoff, 1981), esp. chap. 5, Levinas develops some of these themes. Levinas confined much of his analysis to interhuman relationships. Other scholars have sought to expand his concerns so that something like a "face" can be witnessed in nonhuman others and in places.

We can also see that the modern "turn to the subject" represents a full flowering of the idolatrous impulse because it reduces the world to matter in motion that does not "matter" until we give it significance. The world is defined by its malleability to human design and appropriation. Because this world is without sanctity, it is subject to whatever gaze and intention we bring to it. It has significance insofar as it meets our expectations and satisfies our gaze. The modern account of the world I have developed gives us a picture of nature that is in reality an idol because it remakes the world to reflect and fulfill the desires of our hearts.

The "End" of Idolatry

We should not be surprised that modernity's idolatry has led us to so much moral confusion and worldly destruction. When meaning and significance, and thus also goodness and beauty, become housed in us as value-bestowing subjects, then the only limit to action is a subject's appetite or desire. There is no cosmic or transcendent order to which we are subject. Given that personal desires differ greatly, it is all but inevitable that our idolatries will clash, and that their clash will be realized in soils degraded, waters exhausted, air polluted, plants poisoned, species exterminated, forests felled, animals abused, and other people degraded and exploited. The logic of idolatry demands that the world feed our many appetites, fulfill our hopes, and allay our fears. Armed with the sophisticated powers of instrumental reason and technological innovation, we—those who have these powers—will inevitably remake the world and its people to suit an end alien to their integrity. It becomes necessary that they cease to signify as gifts of God to be cherished and celebrated and instead become commodities confined to the various plays for power, prestige, and comfort.[33]

33. Daniel Bell has helped us see that it is not only material objects that fall within the orbit of commodification, but people as well: "Under capitalism people exist for one another in an instrumental fashion; capitalism encourages us to view others in terms of how they can serve our self-interested projects. In the worst case, people are reified and so become commodities themselves—mere bodies to be exploited or consumed and then discarded; think of slavery, organ mining, or

In a penetrating essay, Bernd Wannenwetsch argues that idolatry, as it has developed within capitalist, market-driven cultures, has led to new forms of human desire that are deeply alienating and destructive. The key to understanding our current situation is not simply that we are constantly being encouraged to desire and covet more things (by being told, for instance, that purchasing this or that product will make us happy or successful or beautiful or . . .), but that we are being encouraged to pursue desire itself as an expression of our freedom and power to pursue whatever we want (because we are the boss!).

> Late capitalism's new economy of desiring, it seems, has outgrown commodity fetishism. The product has been stripped of any promise, functional value, and consumptive or aesthetic pleasure. . . . Since the objects are stripped of their real presence [the products often do not even appear in the ad], robbed of any objective value they would have for themselves, consumption paradoxically has no meaning. The promise of satisfaction is declared void in advance. . . . Shopping is the delightful exposure to commodities of all sorts in the hope that something may eventually stir up our desire. Not that we need anything; but precisely for that reason we desperately need our desire rekindled. The bottom line of this shift is that desire has become self-referential by making itself the object of its own striving: the desire of desire. As such, desire is perceived as the quintessential assurance of our being alive. I desire, therefore I am.[34]

Our situation has become one in which many people, glutted as we are by more commodities than we could possibly appreciate or cherish, are fundamentally bored and profoundly ungrateful (more on this in the final chapter). Do we really think buying yet another product will make us happy? How could that work, given that we are already unsatisfied with the many things we do have? It is thus becoming more and more difficult to get people

---

the sex trade, for example. . . . In a world dominated by commodities, persons come to be valued by the same criteria as commodities—marketability, profitability, and consumability" (*The Economy of Desire: Christianity and Capitalism in a Postmodern World* [Grand Rapids: Baker Academic, 2012], 105–6).

34. Bernd Wannenwetsch, "The Desire of Desire: Commandment and Idolatry in Late Capitalist Societies," in *Idolatry: False Worship in the Bible, Early Judaism and Christianity*, ed. Stephen C. Barton (London: T&T Clark, 2007), 320.

excited to desire anything: the advertisements simply have to become louder and more ridiculous. This is why the focus of advertisers has got to be on getting us excited, getting us to want to desire anything at all. In some cases, it is enough simply to let people know they could buy something *if they wanted to*.[35]

What happens when people lose desire for this world? Forms of disaffection and detachment begin to shape whatever engagement we have with things. Things appear too ordinary or too boring to engage us in deep and meaningful ways. Thomas Carlson has observed that reducing reality's significance to the significance we provide—a reduction that is a hallmark of modernity—"paradoxically entails a hollowing of man and a diminution of the world he encounters. The world now becomes a vast, boring emptiness that offers no possibility that truly grips one's existence, an emptiness or withholding of possibility that tends to yield the obsessive, compensatory, but necessarily self-defeating longing for 'lived experience.'"[36] A world that consists of things in "standing reserve" (Heidegger), or as commodities awaiting appropriation, is also a disenchanted world, an uninteresting world, giving us a restless culture that survives on speed, distraction, and the never-ending pursuit of novelty. This sort of culture yields a world nearly impossible to love because little is deemed worthy of our desire or our cherishing. Being in the world is thus reduced to the state of being comfortably numb.

A world impossible to love! Is this not the clearest sign that an idolatrous disposition inevitably leads to a diseased imagination, an imagination that no longer is able to "know" things as to be protected and nurtured and celebrated? When we appreciate how the idolatrous impulse prevents a loving relationship with others, then we can also see why idolatry represents such a violation of a world created and sustained by God's love. We

35. In *Being Consumed: Economics and Christian Desire* (Grand Rapids: Eerdmans, 2008), William Cavanaugh makes the valuable observation that today's consumer economy wants us to believe that we have the freedom to purchase as we choose (what we purchase does not really matter that much). What is most important is the creation of a subjectivity that believes itself to stand in a lordly position above the world, able to access and purchase it at will and on the chooser's terms.

36. Thomas Carlson, *The Indiscrete Image: Infinitude and Creation of the Human* (Chicago: University of Chicago Press, 2008), 47.

begin to understand why the God who seeks to teach us in the ways of love so detests our idolatrous ways.

It has never been easy to love. Love pursues the freedom and the flourishing of another. It makes room for another so that it can maximally be. It presumes others to be precious and worthy of our attention and care. For that to happen we must learn to see another not as the solution to our anxiety or the fulfillment of our desires, but as the gift that God made him or her to be. The problem is not that we desire. It is that our desire has become degraded by being self-directed. This is why Wannenwetsch says, "Desire as idolatry, desire of desire, however, can only be healed through the creation of *another desire* wrenched from out of itself—a desire that is both strange and natural, that is powerful and genuine as it delights in an object that truly consummates desire instead of deflecting it into self-referential circularity."[37]

It is tempting to think that genuine desire or affection is realized when we become worshipers of nature. But this is not so. To make the trek to beautiful vistas (often at considerable expense) runs the risk of a "green idolatry" in which mountains or lakes or species are commodified to fulfill an aesthetic desire. Too often the nature we seek in a "wilderness experience" is made to fulfill expectations about beauty. That places are beautiful is not the problem. But when we desire our relationship to nature to be mediated by the expectation that only places deemed pretty or spectacular are worthy of our attention, then we do witness an idolatry that condemns much of the world to neglect or even disparagement. What we often fail to realize is that our worship of nature's beauty, especially our designations of certain kinds of landscapes or creatures as beautiful, is also fundamentally a reduction of the world to the expectations that we bring to it. In this reduction great stretches of the world and a multitude of its creatures are abandoned by us as unworthy and thus unlovable.[38]

37. Wannenwetsch, "Desire of Desire," 329 (emphasis original).

38. Cronon argues that a wilderness aesthetic has the effect of making us dismissive, even contemptuous, of humble or ordinary places and experiences. "By teaching us to fetishize sublime places and wild open country, these peculiarly American ways of thinking about wilderness encourage us to adopt too high a standard for what counts as 'natural.' If it isn't hundreds of square miles big, if it

The logic of idolatry is ultimately self- and world-defeating because the idolatrous impulse is born out of ingratitude and anxiety. More specifically, it is born out of a deep distrust in God's power, wisdom, and provision. People embark on an idolatrous path when they believe that God's gifts are not sufficient or God's care misdirected. We begin to think that we must take hold of the world for ourselves. But to do so we must first unmoor others from their life in God so that they can now find their life in us. In this unmooring and remooring, we take the place of God as the ones who determine the value of things. We now determine whatever purpose the world shall serve. Whatever the world is, it now ceases to have a God-given integrity or sanctity.

But why should we trust our ability to give meaning and value to things? Do we not greatly overestimate our intelligence and power when we think we can remake the world into a more suitable, satisfying, or life-giving home? What gradually takes shape as doubt concerning the intelligibility and meaning of the world as we have devised it must finally end in suspicion about the capacity of a form- or meaning-giving subject to prop up and sustain a world. Why should we trust any account of the world's purpose or value if each account is simply a reflection of our various plays for power? Put another way, if the world is itself without significance (remembering that in a nominalist world significance comes along only with us—who are perhaps nothing more than a material machine or a random biological process), why should we put much faith or hope in the subject that is itself the random result of a meaningless world?

Are we condemned to an idolatrous life? Must the world be reduced to the limits of our anxieties, expectations, and desires? Does the world have the capacity to draw us outside of ourselves so that we can see its God-given depth and sanctity? To consider this possibility is to move from an idolatrous relation to the world to an encounter with reality as an icon that opens us to the love of God and the true life of the world. In this movement people are transformed so that wishful thinking and despair are turned to response-ability and delight.

doesn't give us God's-eye views or grand vistas, if it doesn't permit us the illusion that we are alone on the planet, then it really isn't natural. It's too small, too plain, or too crowded to be *authentically* wild" ("Trouble with Wilderness," 86–87).

3

Perceiving Creation

> If the doors of perception were cleansed every thing would appear to man as it is: infinite. For man has closed himself up, till he sees all things thro' narrow chinks of his cavern.
>
> William Blake, *The Marriage of Heaven and Hell*

> What is knowledge? The experience of eternal life. And what is eternal life? The experience of all things in God. For love comes from meeting God. Knowledge united to God fulfills every desire. And for the heart that receives it, it is altogether sweetness overflowing onto the earth. Indeed, there is nothing like the sweetness of God.
>
> Saint Isaac the Syrian, *Ascetic Treatises*

In a letter to his son written near the end of his life, the painter Paul Cézanne reflected on the immense difficulty he was having trying to represent in paint what he was perceiving around himself:

> I must tell you that as a painter I am becoming more clear-sighted before nature, but that with me the realization of my sensations

> is always painful. I cannot attain the intensity that is unfolded before my sense. I have not the magnificent richness of colouring that animates nature. Here on the bank of the river the motifs multiply, the same subject seen from a different angle offers subject for study of the most powerful interest and so varied that I think I could occupy myself for months without changing place, by turning now more to the right, now more to the left.[1]

Though having spent a lifetime developing his powers of attention and perception, Cézanne admits that the world presents him with an intensity and richness of color, light, shape, and texture that he simply cannot convey in his work. How can anyone fully communicate the life and movement and mystery of the world? And so the experience of sensation is accompanied by pain, and the knowledge that despite his best efforts there is an endlessness and depth to the world that will forever elude him. The best that he can do is struggle to bear witness to a world in all its complexity and intricacy and interest. Sometimes this struggle would even take him to an apophatic place, a place of silence and restraint, requiring of him that he leave blank spaces on the canvas so as not to impose a fixed form on a reality that is boundless in its dynamism and points of contact.

The poet Mary Oliver speaks similarly and often about the failure of reason and language to communicate the grace of the world. Though having spent a lifetime attending to the beauties and terrors of the places around her, she hardly knows how to get in the right position to take in what she experiences. Can we be present to others without being an imposition on them? What forms of witness are faithful to what is there before us? Seeing a seal pup on a beach, for instance, she slowly approaches and lies down, her back to the pup. Eventually the pup rolls over, with its side against Oliver's back.

> . . . and so we touched, and maybe
> our breathing together was some kind of heavenly
> conversation

1. Paul Cézanne, *Letters*, ed. John Rewald, trans. Marguerite Kay (New York: Da Capo, 1995), 327, quoted in Douglas E. Christie, *The Blue Sapphire of the Mind: Notes for a Contemplative Ecology* (New York: Oxford University Press, 2013), 172-73.

in God's delicate and magnifying language, the one
we don't dare speak out loud,
not yet.[2]

On seeing roses in some dunes, again she comes close, calms her breathing, and then asks,

Oh sweetness pure and simple, may I join you?

I lie down next to them, on the sand. But to tell
about what happens next, truly I need help.

Will somebody or something please start to sing?[3]

It is as though we first need to listen carefully and patiently for the pulse and song of the world, take its movement deep within our heart and breath, so that we can then imagine and attempt a sympathetic, harmonious sound from out of ourselves.

The testimonies of Cézanne and Oliver demonstrate that we are fooling ourselves if we think that an honest and faithful perception of the world is a simple or automatic thing. Clear, detailed, and deep perceiving requires considerable patience, skill, and commitment. To what extent are people in a position to develop these powers of perception? If we do learn to get close, do we have the appropriate forms to communicate what happens? If our powers of perception are underdeveloped or inadequate, how can we be expected to engage the world as God's creation, or hope to come to what Saint Isaac the Syrian called eternal life, the "experience of all things in God"?

In this chapter we will begin by considering how something like a faithful perception of the world has been rendered more difficult by the practices and patterns of contemporary life. Next, I will develop what can be called an iconic modality of perception, a mode of engagement with the world that is inspired by God's own involvement in the world in the person of Jesus Christ. In calling us to this "iconic" modality I do not mean that we each need formally to join an Orthodox congregation (though we certainly have much to learn from this tradition)

2. Mary Oliver, "The Return," in *What Do We Know: Poems and Prose Poems* (Cambridge, MA: Da Capo, 2002), 9.

3. Oliver, "The Roses," in ibid., 20 (emphasis original).

but rather that we should develop the ascetic disciplines and habits of being that address those passions that prevent us from loving, and thus properly perceiving, others. This iconic modality of approaching and sensing the world represents a reversal of the idolatrous impulse described in the previous chapter, and so makes possible a hospitable embrace of the world. Put summarily, to perceive the world as God's creation, it is crucial that people develop the postures and practices made manifest in Jesus, the true icon of God who reveals to us in his flesh God's way of being with creatures (Col. 1:15).

The Clouding of Perception

The anthropologist Marc Augé has argued that in a time of supermodernity more and more people live in "non-places," meaning that the relationships that bind us to, and hold our interest in, a particular place are being steadily eroded by the goals, speed, and anonymity of today's global economy. Given the transient and frenetic character of so much of life, we have good reason to wonder if boredom and blindness, rather than affection and attention, will be defining features of our age.[4] Though people are physically in the world, they do not often know where they are because their movements take them quickly *across*, rather than patiently *into*, the places of their life.

To appreciate the difference, contrast Cézanne's realization that he could spend months focusing his sensory capacities on the same riverbank with the contemporary experience of harried and hurried workers who spend much of their time in transit, in stores, and in hotels, often glued to a phone or screen. Little real contact, let alone abiding relationship, is possible in this sort of world. When attempts to establish contact are made, they often occur in homogenous, stylized spaces (a strip mall or cookie-cutter housing development) or are met with impersonal, anonymous responses (as from a computer-generated voice). The end result of this situation is that senses deaden and affections wither, even as the volume and pyrotechnics of stimuli increase. Many people are slowly losing the ability to

4. Marc Augé, *Non-Places: An Introduction to an Anthropology of Supermodernity*, 4th ed. (London: Verso, 2008).

feel alive to and inspired by the places in which they move. For them to have to look at a riverbank, even for one hour, could be interpreted only as an invitation to boredom, or perhaps a punishment.

It would be unfair to blame individual people for this development. Massive and systemic changes in culture and economy have made it very unlikely that something like a patient and affectionate attachment to place will occur. Beginning in our education systems, but then continuing in the way we think about professional advancement, the messaging is clear: life is better elsewhere.[5] Neither family, community, nor employers seem to have the power or the attraction to hold individuals in a place. And so people must be ready to move at any moment to seize whatever opportunity comes their way.[6] The end result is that a growing segment of today's population has no idea where they wish to be buried.[7]

Lacking direct, practical, sustained engagement with particular places (and the knowledge that comes from such engagement), consumers in today's global economy find themselves more and more dependent on how the world is presented to them on the world wide web and how it is mediated by marketers, software programmers, app designers, news analysts, and politicians. To consume the world people need to know very little about it. All they need is a credit card and an internet connection. Because so few people have a direct hand in the production of the means of their daily sustenance, it is fair to say that never in history have so many been so ignorant of the contexts and conditions, the vulnerabilities and possibilities, of life.

In 1967 the French critical theorist Guy Debord opened his famous book *The Society of the Spectacle* with these words: "The whole life of those societies in which modern practices of production prevail presents itself as an immense accumulation

5. See the various essays in *Rooted in the Land: Essays on Community and Place*, ed. William Vitek and Wes Jackson (New Haven: Yale University Press, 1996), esp. Eric Zencey, "The Rootless Professors."

6. The sociologist Zygmunt Bauman traces several of these developments in *Liquid Modernity* (Cambridge: Polity, 2000) and *Liquid Love* (Cambridge: Polity, 2003).

7. For an insightful discussion on why this matters, see Robert Pogue Harrison, *The Dominion of the Dead* (Chicago: University of Chicago Press, 2003).

of *spectacles*. All that once was lived directly has become mere representation."[8] By the "spectacle" Debord did not only mean an image, but the power of consumer and media outlets to shape human life around the acquisition of commodities and images. Simply by purchasing the right clothes or driving the right car one could display one's identification with a social or economic class and the image it signified. Debord believed that the character of human relationships was being fundamentally altered by the spectacle as people were becoming more passive and subject to various forms of market manipulation. An image of life, as presented in various forms of mass advertising campaigns, had come to shape how life is imagined and pursued.

Debord argued that human life had become impoverished and rendered inauthentic by these images because the acquisition of commodities now supplanted relationships with people and places. In the age of the spectacle, the value of things is determined by how well they can be made to be emblematic of a particular style. Who people are is a matter not of *being* a certain kind of person but of *having* the kinds of commodities that will give the *appearance* of a particular kind of persona or image. The shift from being to having to appearing is momentous because it leads to the diminishment of the capacity of people to engage the life of the world.[9] In the society of the spectacle, people see an image of what they like and then alter themselves and their world—normally by shopping—to try to match the image. According to Debord, mass-media marketing had taken the place of religion because the inspiration and goals

8. Guy Debord, *The Society of the Spectacle*, trans. Donald Nicholson-Smith (New York: Zone Books, 1994), 12 (emphasis original).

9. In *The Postmodern Turn* (New York: Guilford Press, 1997), Steven Best and Douglas Kellner give the following helpful summary:

> For Debord, the spectacle is a tool of pacification and depoliticization; it is a "permanent opium war" that stupefies social subjects and distracts them from the most urgent task of real life: recovering the full range of their human powers through creative practice. In Debord's formulation, the concept of the spectacle is integrally connected to the concept of separation, for in passively consuming spectacles, one is separated from other people and from actively producing one's life. Capitalist society separates workers from the product of their labor, art from life, and spheres of production from consumption, all of which involve spectators passively observing the products of social life. (84)

of practical life now circulated around possibilities offered in stores rather than in a church.

Since the time of Debord's writing, a great deal has happened to exacerbate the conditions of alienation he described. With the development of web-based shopping, social media, and a plethora of information/infotainment outlets, people can now tailor their experience of the world to an image of the life they want to have. If you don't like how the news is being presented on PBS, no problem. You can easily switch to Fox News or Al Jazeera. Material imperfections of color and shape can easily be adjusted at the click of a mouse or the sweep of an airbrush. At the same time, technological devices of all kinds are being steadily invented to give us experiences of the world on demand and as we desire. If you don't like seeing homeless people, no problem. Contact lenses are being developed that will make them disappear from view. The cultural critic Evgeny Morozov writes,

> Even boredom seems to be in its last throes: designers in Japan have found a way to make our train trips perpetually fun-filled. With the help of an iPhone, a projector, a GPS module and Microsoft's Kinect motion sensor, their contrivance allows riders to add new objects to what they see "outside," thus enlivening the bleak landscape in their train windows. This could be a big hit in North Korea—and not just on trains.[10]

Media platforms and technological devices are not simply neutral tools that we use to move through life. Their power is much more extensive, because they shape and frame what we perceive and understand the world to be. When people spend enough time in front of screens, it becomes all but inevitable that the whole world takes on the character of something to be watched. Given the technologies we now have for manipulating screens in whatever fashion we like to suit our own particular tastes, if we find the *Mona Lisa* boring, no problem. We can run the image through the Fatify app or add the graphics and colors we like to make it amusing or better than the original!

10. Evgeny Morozov, "The Perils of Perfection," in *New York Times Sunday Review*, March 2, 2013 (http://www.nytimes.com/2013/03/03/opinion/sunday/the-perils-of-perfection.html?_r=0). Thanks to Elliott Haught for alerting me to Morozov's work in his 2014 Duke Divinity School master's thesis, "Devices and Discipleship: On Living Faithfully in the Digital Age."

Should we be surprised that people often find the world uninteresting and dull?

Technological devices also have tremendous power to shape who we are as people. Consider the idea at work in an app like Seesaw. This app enables its users to crowdsource decisions, meaning you can run instant polls of your friends to get advice on what to buy, where to live, and what to do. Again, Morozov: "Seesaw offers an interesting twist on how we think about feedback and failure. It used to be that we bought things to impress our friends, fully aware that they might not like our purchases. Now this logic is inverted: if something impresses our friends, we buy it. The risks of rejection have been minimized; we know well in advance how many Facebook 'likes' our every decision would accumulate."[11] Silicon Valley's engineers and programmers (and their well-funded backers) aim to give us a "frictionless future," a world that is without opacity, ambiguity, and imperfection. This is a world in which the ideas of human agency and responsibility, and the skills of attention and affection, are fundamentally transformed.[12] This is a world remade to match the desires and expectations we have (or are encouraged by marketers and gurus to have).

My point is not to say that all technological innovations and devices are uniformly bad. It is, rather, to note how the experience of reality can be transformed such that, rather than experiencing "all things in God," and as part of a divine drama moving toward the reconciliation of all things, we increasingly experience "ourselves in all things." To live in today's

11. Morozov, "Perils of Perfection."

12. In *To Save Everything, Click Here: The Folly of Technological Solutionism* (New York: Public Affairs, 2013), Morozov says,

> Imperfection, ambiguity, opacity, disorder, and the opportunity to err, sin, to do the wrong thing: all of these are constitutive of human freedom, and any concentrated attempt to root them out will root out that freedom as well. If we don't find the strength and the courage to escape the silicon mentality that fuels much of the current quest for technological perfection, we risk finding ourselves with a politics devoid of everything that makes politics desirable, with humans who have lost their basic capacity for moral reasoning, with lackluster (if not moribund) cultural institutions that don't take risks and only care about their financial bottom lines, and, most terrifyingly, with a perfectly controlled social environment that would make dissent not just impossible but possibly even unthinkable. (xii)

media-saturated, consumer-oriented world means that what the world *is*—how it signifies and what value it bears—is becoming more and more a reflection of how we want the world to be. Why live in the world as given, or commit to the nurture and healing of a wounded world, when we can instead live within a simulated version of it, a version in which we can set the terms of our living?[13]

In the previous chapter I suggested that in the time of industrial, technological, and consumerist modernity, idolatry has become the dominant mode of perception. By *idolatry* I did not simply mean the fabrication of statues or monuments to our own self-glorification, though there is ample evidence of that. I meant, rather, a form of perception (and thus also a capacity for apprehension) in which what is seen reflects the ambition, anxiety, insecurity, hubris—the deep desire—of the one perceiving. To gaze at things idolatrously is to put in motion ways of naming and narration—and thus also practical and economic forms of engagement with the world—that establish us as the centers and bestowers of value and significance. This is why Jean-Luc Marion says idols function as mirrors reflecting the scope of the viewer's aim. In an idolatrous context we cannot see things as they are. We see them for what we desire them to be. Our situation is made all the more difficult by the fact that we are mostly oblivious to the idolatrous, mirrorlike character of the seeing we do. The effect of so much of our culture's training is to convince us that we really are the center around which the world moves.[14]

13. The French social theorist Jean Baudrillard argued in books like *Simulacra and Simulation* that the power of simulation had become so great that people could no longer distinguish between reality and illusion. Postmodernity, for him, is the time in which the distinction between reality and unreality has been erased. As Best and Kellner note, "In a hyperreal postmodern world, reality is dissipated and depleted; it loses its power and force through its cultural processing, through mechanical reproduction and the proliferation of illusions and pseudo-forms" (*Postmodern Turn*, 102).

14. The anthropologist Thomas de Zengotita, in *Mediated: How the Media Shapes Your World and the Way You Live in It* (New York: Bloomsbury, 2005), describes the aim of modernity as the replacing of God with the "Me" who expects the fulfillment of every desire. No matter where this "Me" looks, it can now expect to find politicians, marketers, teachers, preachers seeking to please. "They want you reclining there, on the anonymous side of the screen, while they

Is a nonidolatrous form of perception possible? I believe this is a critical question, because what is at stake is the truth of the world and the possibility of our being able to live responsibly and faithfully within it. Idolatry is destroying our world. It is destroying our fields and watersheds, just as it is destroying our neighborhoods and families, because it replaces a vision of how God wants the world to be with a vision for how we want it to be. Idolatry undermines the possibility that we might live fully into ourselves as creatures made by God to love each other, and in doing so experience and contribute to the goodness and beauty of all that God has made.

One major reason the idolatrous impulse is so dangerous is that it makes fidelity to others nearly impossible. To see what I mean, consider Wendell Berry's account of the farmer who has just purchased a new section of land. A good farmer will take time to determine what the limits and potential of the land are and then work carefully so as to enhance its potential and minimize its damage. She will see, for instance, that the pasture can sustain only a small herd. To add more, perhaps with the hope of increased profit, would be to injure the field and compromise its carrying capacity. The temptation is to come to the land with all kinds of expectations and dreams of what the land will do for her, and thus violate the limits and the possibilities that are genuinely within it. In other words, the danger is that the farmer will see the land not for what it is but for what she wishes it to be.[15]

The situation here is not unlike that of the newly married groom or bride who comes to the marriage with an idealized picture of his or her new spouse. The problem is that no spouse can, or should, live up to another's ideal, because the aim of marital love is to welcome the other as the unique person that he or she is. The work of marriage is to come into the presence of each other so that each can help the other develop to full

parade before you, purveyors of every conceivable blandishment, every form of pleasure, every kind of comfort and consolation, every kind of thrill, every kind of provocation—anything you want. You're the customer, after all, you're the voter, you're the reader, you're the viewer—you're the boss" (268).

15. Wendell Berry, "People, Land, and Community," in *The Art of the Commonplace: The Agrarian Essays of Wendell Berry*, ed. Norman Wirzba (Washington, DC: Counterpoint, 2002), 186–87.

potential and overcome his or her failings. Fidelity disappears when a spouse does not recognize, honor, and nurture the other so that the other can maximally be himself or herself. The marriage is bound to wither and fail so long as the spouses remain committed to the *idea* they have of each other and do not see each other for who they are.

How is fidelity to be achieved? By developing appropriate forms of discipline. Berry describes the discipline of good farming in the following way:

> If one's sight is clear and if one stays on and works well, one's love gradually responds to the place as it really is, and one's visions gradually image possibilities that are really in it. Vision, possibility, work, and life—*all* have changed by mutual correction. Correct discipline, given enough time, gradually removes one's self from one's line of sight. One works to better purpose then and makes fewer mistakes, because at last one sees where one is. Two human possibilities of the highest order thus come within reach: what one wants can become the same as what one has, and one's knowledge can cause respect for what one knows.[16]

Discipline is the key because it is in the daily work of taming one's ambition and cultivating the skills of care and compassion that an embrace of the world in its grace and depth becomes possible. The discipline talked about here is not unlike the posture that Mary Oliver seeks, an embodied posture in which people move close so as to listen, and then carefully respond in sympathy and harmony with the world around. As we will soon see, the Christian name for this discipline is discipleship.

Iconic Perception?

It is now time to develop an "iconic" form and mode of perception. By iconic I mean a perceptive approach to things in which others are not reduced to the scope of utilitarian and instrumental aims. In this mode of perception, people are called to open themselves to the integrity and sanctity of the world,

16. Ibid., 187.

what William Blake once called the world's holiness.[17] What is seen in an iconic mode is not the effect and fulfillment of the gazer's desire, because in an icon we are presented with a depth and transcendence that overwhelms us and calls into question the expectations through which we approached it in the first place. In the welcome of this overwhelming, a new form of subjectivity begins to take shape.

Marion says that in iconic seeing the invisible saturates the visible, giving to what is seen a depth and immensity that eludes capture. "The icon summons the gaze to surpass itself by never freezing on a visible. . . . The gaze can never rest or settle if it looks at an icon; it always must rebound upon the visible, in order to go back in it up the infinite stream of the invisible. In this sense, the icon makes visible only by giving rise to an infinite gaze."[18] This gaze is infinite because in the icon we are invited to look beyond its surface features to an excess of meaning and significance that is inspired and nourished by the infinite God who calls it into being. No meaning that we could give exhausts the other, and so all perception is an invitation to depth, a call to look with greater patience, attentiveness, and love. As Marion notes elsewhere, when we recognize that we cannot assign "a single meaning to the immensity of lived experiences," then a "hermeneutic without end" is put in motion, a hermeneutic that constitutes us as bearing testimony to a world that exceeds comprehension. We are no longer transcendental egos constituting the world. Instead, we are witnesses constituted by what happens to us.[19]

Iconic perception teaches that love is the crucial and most authentic movement of seeing. Why? Because love, when it is true, resists and refuses the idolatrous impulse. Love does not pretend to comprehend, nor does it mean to take the other as a possession or object of control. Love begins with the acknowledgment of another's integrity, and proceeds with a disposition

17. In *The Marriage of Heaven and Hell*, Blake says, "For every thing that lives is holy" (in *The Complete Poetry and Prose of William Blake*, ed. David V. Erdman, rev. ed. [New York: Doubleday, 1988], 45). In this same work he affirms the divine presence at work in creation by observing that "Energy is Eternal Delight" (34).

18. Jean-Luc Marion, *God without Being* (Chicago: University of Chicago Press, 1991), 18.

19. Jean-Luc Marion, *In Excess: Studies of Saturated Phenomena* (New York: Fordham University Press, 2002), 112–13.

of fidelity in the face of surprise, bewilderment, and unknowing. To look with the power of love is to want to see another in all of the other's uniqueness and particularity. How often do we pause and stand amazed before the unique mystery that another is? Love is the welcoming and hospitable gesture that makes oneself available to others, sets them free to be themselves, and nourishes them in the ways of life. As the apostle Paul put it, love "does not insist on its own way," but instead "bears all things, believes all things, hopes all things, endures all things. Love never ends" (1 Cor. 13:5–8). Iconic seeing never ends because the divine love that founds the world is inexhaustible in its variety and extent. To try to match it with our speech or representations would take forever.

The movement from idolatrous to iconic seeing is, as we shall see, anything but easy, because what is at stake (and in question) is our presumed position in the world. If idols and icons establish what we perceive the being of things to be, they also express our manner of being in the world. For instance, to see the world around us primarily as a warehouse or store of "consumable goods" presupposes that we understand ourselves to be shoppers who move through this world with the ignorance and ease of the credit card swipe. Things are presented/marketed to us as commodities that are more or less desirable. We covet the role of ourselves as sovereign agents who have the freedom to select from among these commodities and who, in making these selections, construct the identities we desire.[20] Shopping can thus represent a way of being in the world that secures personal prestige, comfort, convenience, and control. Why would anyone want to give up a way of being in the world in which we have to know and do so little to get so much?

To recognize that our ways of seeing grow out of and perpetuate ways of being in the world is also to recognize that a transformation of vision goes hand in hand with a transformation of life. To move from an idolatrous to an iconic way of

20. In *Being Consumed: Economics and Christian Desire* (Grand Rapids: Eerdmans, 2008), William Cavanaugh shows that in a consumerist world the freedom achieved has the effect of further separating people from the world in which they consume. The freedom at work is the ability not simply to purchase something (and thus perhaps claim responsibility for it) but to stand above the world as the one who could always choose otherwise.

seeing requires that we approach, apprehend, and engage the world around us in fundamentally different ways. Put simply, we cannot learn to perceive the world *as God's creation* if we do not at the same time also learn to live in ways that make that kind of perception possible.

Seeing creation is no small or easy thing, because much more is at stake than a few ideas about how we think the world began. Viewed biblically, the term "creation" designates a moral and spiritual topography that situates all things in relationship with each other and with God. That means the teaching of creation is about the "character" of the world and the health of the relationships that are operative within it. As Paul Blowers has recently shown, among early church writers creation was understood in an expansive way as the cosmic sweep of God's redemptive activity. As such, creation was a Triune act and could not be understood apart from the work of Christ and the Holy Spirit to lead creation toward its fulfillment and perfection.[21] To commit to seeing the world *as creation*, therefore, had the practical effect of calling people to *participate* in God's redemptive work.

It is an act of faith and love to see the world in this way, because what we are doing, in the most basic sense, is engaging the world in ways that do not insist on our own way. Why? Because God's ways with the world are believed to be prior and determinative, and because God's love is utterly noncoercive, enabling creatures to move into the fullness of their life. Faith, to slightly modify a formulation by Hans Urs von Balthasar, is the willingness to allow God's love both in and for the world to have its way.[22] It is to allow this creative love to inspire, shape, and direct our love in the world. To believe that the world is

21. Blowers observes that "the conviction of many patristic interpreters was that the advent of Christ inaugurates the new, eschatological creation where the gracious, intimate presence of the Creator in and with the creation will finally be manifested as 'all in all' (1 Cor. 15:28)" (*Drama of the Divine Economy: Creator and Creation in Early Christian Theology and Piety* [Oxford: Oxford University Press, 2012], 2). Because creation is a Triune act, "The Spirit was ever at work in constituting, animating, sanctifying, beautifying, and consummating creation—in ways believed to be a cooperation in, and completion of, the work of the Father and the Son" (14).

22. Hans Urs von Balthasar, *The Glory of the Lord: A Theological Aesthetics*, vol. 7, *Theology: The New Covenant* (San Francisco: Ignatius, 1989), 401.

creation is, therefore, an act in which we discover ourselves constituted *as creatures* to live into our relationships with others in ways that testify to the divine love everywhere already at work in the world. When we learn to love as God loves, our perception is changed because we now encounter and respond to others so as to nurture them in their life. As I develop my account of disciplined perception, I will draw from the traditions of iconography and monasticism, since both are schools devoted to the correction and instruction of Christian vision. But first, a look at Scripture.

Biblical scholar Ellen Davis says that the moments are rare in the Bible when an author takes us into God's experience of seeing the world: "Biblical narrative usually confines itself to externals; it tells us what a character (including God) said or did. Only occasionally does it move inside the eyes, to tell us what and how someone saw, and when it does so, the specific perception is important."[23] One of these unusual moments occurs at the very beginning when we as readers are given a glimpse of how God sees creation as it is being made. As we have yet to discover, what gives the world its character *as creation* is precisely that God sees it in a particular way.[24]

The Genesis 1 poem is regularly punctuated with the refrain, "And God saw that it was good" (1:4, 10, 12, 18, 21, 25). Verse 31 repeats and emphasizes the refrain as a summative assessment: "God saw everything that he had made, and indeed, it was very good." Creation's goodness—its beauty and splendor, the very quality about it that makes God pause to behold it in moments of rapt attention and appreciation—is a reflection of God's perception of it. Far from simply being a fact about the world, the world's goodness—its character and what establishes it as God's creation—stems from God's way of approaching and engaging the world. But for us to try to perceive as God does involves a double seeing: God sees

23. Ellen F. Davis, *Scripture, Culture, and Agriculture: An Agrarian Reading of the Bible* (New York: Cambridge University Press, 2009), 46.

24. Another key passage illuminating how God perceives creation can be found in God's two speeches to Job in Job 38–41. What emerges is God's detailed, attentive regard for the great breadth and depth of creation. God clearly delights in creatures, even those—like the mighty Behemoth and Leviathan—having the power to crush humans.

the creature made, but also the divine creative work that is bringing it into beautiful being. God, in other words, in seeing a creature also sees the divine *creativity* and *intention* that makes and lets it be.

To appreciate more deeply God's mode of perception we need to attend to what happens on the seventh day. Looking out onto that first Sabbath sunrise, God sees the hospitable love that "makes room" for what is not God to be and to flourish. Divine love is the action that brings creation into being, which means that *God sees each creature and his own love at the same time*.[25] Seeing the night and the day, the water and the dry land, the fish of the sea and the birds of the air, and the creeping things and wild animals of the earth, God also sees the divine love that desires each and every thing to be the unique thing that it is. In other words, a tree, when seen by God, is never simply a vertical log with varying kinds of foliage or some amount of lumber. A tree is also, and more fundamentally, an incarnation of God's love—made visible, tactile, and fragrant as a giant redwood or cedar of Lebanon. Perceiving the diverse forms of creation *and* the love that holds and sustains them in their being, God "rests."

God's *shabbat* has nothing to do with God being tired or worn out from the labor of creating. Instead it points to the delight God finds in beholding the world, and the delight God expresses in loving the world into being. God's rest, quite unlike our own, is not a means of escape from the pressures and strains of the world. It couldn't be, because God's world is saturated and sustained by love, and love results in *relationship* rather than alienation, *hospitality* rather than separation. God's rest is a perfect, affirming presence to the world, a presence in which others are fully acknowledged and embraced as good and beautiful. In genuine *shabbat* there is no restlessness at all because there is no other place one could possibly want to be, no other thing one could possibly want to have (restlessness can here be defined as the inability or refusal to love and be

25. There is widespread agreement within theological traditions that God does not create out of necessity but *ex nihilo* and in freedom and as an act of love. God's Triune life, in turn, is the lens through which the meaning of this creative love is brought to light. Following Irenaeus (*Against Heresies* 4), one can say that God the Father creates with "two hands": through/by the Son and in the Holy Spirit.

grateful for where and who one is and whom one is with).[26] To be in a Sabbath frame of heart is to be able to find a riverbank worthy of a lifetime's attention and care because one now sees in it the love of God at work. Is it possible to be tired or bored with God's love?

Sabbath seeing is iconic seeing, because in it the love that creates the world and the love that connects the perceiver to it are joined. Our loving attention, in other words, meets God's loving intention in an unending movement of call and response.[27] Here the gaze becomes infinite as one enters the streams of life made perpetually fresh by God's inexhaustible love (think here of Paul's astonishment at the unsearchable, forever-deepening love of God as expressed at the end of Romans 8). In this modality one sees more fully—but never comprehensively—what is there to see by *giving oneself* to the divine love at work within and around it.[28]

Giving oneself to what one sees is the heart of iconic perception, because it is in self-giving that we communicate our commitment to engage another *as other*, rather than as the object of our own desires. In this context, it is important to underscore that from a theological point of view, icons have their true sense only in the liturgical contexts of worship and service. Icons are not pretty pictures to be painted and looked at. Léonid

26. I have developed these themes in *Living the Sabbath: Discovering the Rhythms of Rest and Delight* (Grand Rapids: Brazos, 2006).

27. Think here of Jean-Louis Chrétien's description of the "call" of beauty: "What is beautiful is what calls out by manifesting itself and manifests itself by calling out. To draw us to itself as such, to put us in motion toward it, to move us, to come and find us where we are so that we will seek it—such is beauty's call and such is our vocation" (*The Call and the Response*, trans. Anne A. Davenport [New York: Fordham University Press, 2004], 9). God makes a good and beautiful work and then, as the wide sweep of Scripture unfolds, commits to "being with" creatures as their nurturing and healing source. This divine movement of attending to beauty thus acts as the basic inspiration for our own attending to the world.

28. Chrétien says that in the self-giving response to the call of another a prophetic form of subjectivity is born in which another is enabled to speak through me: "The prophetic body becomes a musical body and resounds with a harmony that is no longer human. The prophet is no longer so much a speech-bearer as a voice-bearer. Whereas we bear the other's speech only in our speech, in the prophetic case the prophet's own speech disappears. He only seems to be speaking: his voice no longer belongs to him but constitutes a medium for the other" (ibid., 26).

Ouspensky, one of the great scholars of the icon, says, "The icon never strives to stir the emotions of the faithful. Its task is not to provoke in them one or another natural human emotion, but to guide every emotion as well as the reason and all the other faculties of human nature on the way towards transfiguration."[29] The icon is a means of prayer, an exercise in self-detachment, which leads people to seeing every created thing anew because in an icon's veneration disciples are invited to see the world in its divine light, bathed in God's transfiguring love.

Sabbath seeing thus gives rise to a way of being in the world in which perceivers acknowledge and delight in the beauty of the world, even as they recognize and participate in the divine love that animates what is there to behold. To move into Sabbath rest, we are instructed to begin by stopping our activity, if only because so much of what we do amounts to a denial or denigration of God's love and beauty at work in the world. It amounts to the forcing of others to suit our idolatrous impulses. For us to observe Sabbath is, therefore, to try to see and love the world the way God does. It is to make ourselves available to and responsible for the grandeur of God's work. When we see others in ways that participate in God's way of seeing, we practice the kind of hospitality in which the agendas I might have for another are replaced with the desire to address another's need and help the other achieve his or her divinely given potential.[30]

Sabbath teaching builds upon the crucial theological insight that God and creatures exist in a noncompetitive relationship with each other. Being in a noncompetitive relationship means (a) that creatures and God do not exist on the same plane or

29. Léonid Ouspensky, "The Meaning and Language of Icons," in *The Meaning of Icons*, ed. Léonid Ouspensky and Vladimir Lossky (Crestwood, NY: St. Vladimir's Seminary Press, 1982), 39.

30. This point needs emphasis because it is often, and mistakenly, assumed that God's creation of the world *ex nihilo* represents God's imposition upon creatures or God's exercise of power over creatures. As such, creation is not the reflection of a hospitable God "making room" for others to be themselves (as early church writers often assumed). For a more carefully nuanced account of how creation *ex nihilo* is an exercise of noncoercive love, see Rowan Williams's essay "On Being Creatures," in *On Christian Theology* (Oxford: Blackwell, 2000). Blowers argues that the fundamental error of those who see *creatio ex nihilo* as a violent act is that they fail to see matter as the reflection of God's graciousness and as a vital element within God's economy of salvation (*Drama of the Divine Economy*, 354–55).

level of reality (this, in large part, is what the teaching of *creation ex nihilo*, or creation from nothing, means to express), and therefore (b) that creatures do not have to become small for God to be great (nor is God in any way diminished by the success or full flowering of creatures). Because God and creatures do not compete for reality, God can be present to each creature as its nurturing and healing power. It follows, then, that God's glory is amplified the more each creature lives fully into the divine love at work within it. We, in turn, give glory to God by participating in God's nurturing and healing ways with the world.

The Gospels contain multiple accounts in which an iconic form of perception can be observed. Consider the following characterization of Jesus's mode of perception: "Then Jesus went about all the cities and villages, teaching in their synagogues, and proclaiming the good news of the kingdom, and curing every disease and every sickness. When he saw the crowds, he had compassion for them, because they were harassed and helpless, like sheep without a shepherd" (Matt. 9:35-36; cf. Mark 6:34). When in Luke 7:12–15 Jesus sees the widow who has just lost her son, he has compassion and raises her dead son. When in John 5:2–9 Jesus sees the man who has been an invalid for thirty-eight years, he approaches him and heals him. Over and over again we see that Jesus never simply sees others as the surface beings that they are. He sees beyond the surface and into the creative, enlivening love at work within them. When that love, and all the potential life that love represents, is stifled or thwarted by hunger or disease or alienation or demon possession, Jesus addresses it by feeding, healing, comforting, and exorcising the demons of those wounded. His seeing and response—the compassionate response being the clearest indication that iconic seeing has occurred—is a joining with the divine love always already at work within creatures. By ministering to others, Jesus's love comes into harmonious alignment with the divine love that first brought creatures into being and daily sustains them.

Recall too that Jesus is understood to be the lord of the Sabbath (see Matt. 12:8; Mark 2:28; and Luke 6:5). This means that in his life and ministry we are able to see what the full realization of Sabbath observance practically looks like. Like

God the Father, who in the creation of the world witnesses to its goodness, beauty, and love, so too Jesus the Son witnesses to creation's loveliness and worth by extending the love that liberates and nourishes creatures to maximally be themselves. Jesus never sees others as what they currently are: degraded by sin and frustrated in their ability to be what God has made uniquely possible in them. Instead he sees them in terms of what they could be if God's love within them were set free and fully activated. Jesus, we could say, using the language of iconography, sees everyone and everything as already transfigured by God's love.[31] Or, drawing on Pauline language, Jesus sees everyone as the "new creation" that he or she can become by being in Christ (2 Cor. 5:17).

Drawing on the Iconographic Tradition

What makes iconic seeing possible at all? This question cannot be taken for granted, especially when we remember that in the church's history there have been vigorous attacks against icons and all that they represent. We need to be clear about what iconic seeing is and what it is not. To start, it is not at all or in any way a seeing of God's eternal and ineffable essence. Consider here the work of John of Damascus, one of the earliest and most able defenders of icons. In his *Three Treatises on the Divine Images* he says over and over again that the iconographic image points to the archetype without in any way being that archetype. There is an abyss between Creator and creation, which means

31. Ouspensky writes, "The beauty of the visible world lies not in the transitory splendor of its present state, but in the very meaning of its existence, in its coming transfiguration laid down in it as a possibility to be realized by man. In other words, beauty is holiness, and its radiance the participation of the creature in Divine Beauty" ("Meaning and Language of Icons," 35). Developing this point further: "All the visible world represented in the icon changes, becomes the image of the future unity of the whole creation—the Kingdom of the Holy Spirit. In accordance with this, all that is depicted in the icon reflects not the disorder of our sinful world, but divine order, peace, a realm governed not by earthly logic, not by human morality, but by divine grace. It is the new order in the new creation" (40–41). Pavel Florensky, another of the great thinkers on the meaning of icons, says, "The icon is the image of the future age," because in it we are called to glimpse each creature in its fully realized, God-created beauty ("On the Icon," *Eastern Churches Review* 8 [1976]: 11–36, quote on 30).

that everything material, though participating in God as the source of its life, is never to be identified with God.

Also of great importance is John of Damascus's insistence that the veneration of icons does not amount to the worship of matter because God alone is to be worshiped.

> I do not venerate matter, I venerate the fashioner of matter, who became matter for my sake and accepted to dwell in matter and through matter worked my salvation, and I will not cease from reverencing matter, through which my salvation was worked. . . . I reverence the rest of matter and hold in respect that through which my salvation came, because it is filled with divine energy and grace.[32]

Two matters of importance need elaboration: first, that icons are made possible by the incarnation of God in the flesh of Jesus Christ; and second, that matter is filled with what has been called the "divine energies."

Defenders of icons have long noted that to attack the possibility of an icon is also to attack the incarnation that is the heart and blood of Christian faith. It is, in principle, to deny that Jesus was fully human, fully flesh, and fully divine. It is to succumb to the gnostic, Docetic, or Manichaean temptations that would have us deny that matter could ever be a suitable home for the divine life. John of Damascus is clear that if God did not enter into matter, then matter cannot be taken up into God: "I venerate the Creator, created for my sake, who came down to his creation without being lowered or weakened, that he might glorify my nature and bring about communion with the divine nature."[33] Entering into flesh does not suddenly make flesh divine: "For the nature of the flesh did not become divinity, but as the Word became flesh immutably, remaining what it was, so also the flesh became the Word without losing what it was, being rather made equal to the Word hypostatically."[34]

32. Saint John of Damascus, *Three Treatises on the Divine Images*, trans. Andrew Louth (Crestwood, NY: St. Vladimir's Seminary Press, 2003), 29 (treatise 1.16). In treatise 2.14 he says that matter is not to be reverenced as if it were God but "as filled with divine energy and grace" (71).

33. Ibid., 22 (treatise 1.4).

34. Ibid., 86 (treatise 3.6).

A vision of salvation as *theosis* sits behind this way of thinking. *Theosis*, or deification in Christ, assumes that God became a human being so that human beings can participate in the divine life. This teaching has roots that extend deeply in the writings of the early church. Tertullian, for instance, wrote: "God lived with men as man that man might be taught to live the divine life: God lived on man's level that man might be able to live on God's level."[35] Clement of Alexandria said that God became man so that we might learn from a man "how it may be that man should become God."[36] But it is Vladimir Lossky who has recently defended this vision most clearly. As he presents it, for human beings to participate in the divine nature does not mean that God's transcendence and God's ineffable nature have thereby been reduced. To see how this is possible we need to distinguish between God's *essence*, which is forever unknowable and inaccessible, and God's *energies*, which are the divine operations that go forth from God and communicate God in the world. These energies are not creatures but God himself (though not according to God's substance) and flow eternally from the one essence that the Trinity is. "In the order of the economic manifestation of the Trinity in the world, all energy originates in the Father, being communicated by the Son in the Holy Spirit."[37]

The distinction between God's essence and energies is important because our union with God, our participation in God's life, is a participation in God's energies rather than God's essence. "The union to which we are called is neither hypostatic—as in the case of the human nature of Christ—nor substantial,

35. *Adversus Marcionem* 2.27, quoted in Graham Ward, *Christ and Culture* (Oxford: Blackwell, 2005), 5.

36. *Protrepicus* 1.8.4, quoted in Ward, *Christ and Culture*, 5. Two very helpful books elaborating the theme of *theosis* in the patristic period are Panayiotis Nellas, *Deification in Christ: Orthodox Perspectives on the Nature of the Human Person* (Crestwood, NY: St. Vladimir's Seminary Press, 1987), and Geōrgios I. Mantzaridēs, *The Deification of Man: Saint Gregory Palamas and the Orthodox Tradition* (Crestwood, NY: St. Vladimir's Seminary Press, 1984). For a recent, ecumenical assessment see Michael Christensen and Jeffery Wittung, eds., *Partakers of the Divine Nature: The History and Development of Deification in the Christian Traditions* (Grand Rapids: Baker Academic, 2007).

37. Vladimir Lossky, *The Mystical Theology of the Eastern Church* (Crestwood, NY: St. Vladimir's Seminary Press, 1997), 82.

as in that of the three divine Persons: it is union with God in His energies, or union by grace making us participate in the divine nature, without our essence becoming thereby the essence of God."[38] This means that we remain as creatures while becoming God by grace, or as John of Damascus put it succinctly, "What is deified does not become God by nature, but by participation."[39]

Why does this discussion of the divine energies matter? Because it helps us understand that from the beginning God has desired to be "with us" as God Emmanuel, that God has been communicating himself in the broad sweep of history that goes from creation to consummation, and that God wants us to share and participate in the divine life and love that is the source of all being, goodness, and beauty. God does not simply want to be beheld (or feared) by us. The astounding thing is that God wants to be our companion (see John 15, where God's followers are called friends) and wants us to share in God's life as the way of love, joy, and peace. God's energies have come to their fullest and most poignant expression in the person of Jesus of Nazareth, but this divine energy radiates throughout the whole creation. As Lossky puts it, "The divine energies are within everything and outside everything."[40]

The basis for this way of speaking is again christological. Beginning with John's Gospel, Christians have described Jesus as the eternal, creating Word. "All things came into being through him, and without him not one thing came into being" (John 1:3). In the Christ hymn of Colossians the language of Christ as the creator and redeemer of all creation is put in equally striking terms: "He is the image [icon] of the invisible God, the

38. Ibid., 87.

39. Saint John of Damascus, *Three Treatises*, 33 (treatise 1.19). Ouspensky ("Meaning and Language of Icons") gives another helpful way of describing what happens to human nature in *theosis*:

> Human nature remains what it is—the nature of a creature; but his person, his hypostasis, by acquiring the grace of the Holy Spirit, by this very fact associates itself with Divine Life, thus changing the very being of its creaturely nature. The grace of the Holy Spirit penetrates into his nature, combines with it, fills and transfigures it. Man grows, as it were, into the eternal life, already acquiring here on earth the beginning of this life, the beginning of deification, which will be made fully manifest in the life to come. (34–35)

40. Lossky, *Mystical Theology of the Eastern Church*, 89.

firstborn of all creation; for in him all things in heaven and on earth were created, things visible and invisible, whether thrones or dominions or rulers or powers—all things have been created through him and for him. He himself is before all things, and in him all things hold together" (Col. 1:15–17).

As reflection on this theme developed, it became clear that it is a major mistake to think of creation apart from Christ. Saint Athanasius argued that no part of creation is ever without Jesus as the eternal Word of God. "The Self-revealing of the Word is in every dimension—above, in creation; below, in the Incarnation; in the depth, in Hades; in the breadth, throughout the world. All things have been filled with the knowledge of God."[41] The incarnate Word is present everywhere, ordering, directing, and giving life to all things, yet being contained by no single thing. Christ is the Word through whom all things come to be and through whom all things will be renewed and redeemed, for Christ shows that there is no inconsistency between the creation of things and their salvation. Though the Word entered into flesh at a particular time in the person of Jesus, the eternal, immaterial Word was not far from creatures before then, "for no part of creation had ever been without Him Who, while ever abiding in union with the Father, yet fills all things that are."[42]

Athanasius clearly understands creation as the expression of God's Word at work within it. The great error is to think we can see creation properly without also seeing the Word that informs and directs it. Perceiving the pleasure that is possible by immersing oneself in the material world, we are in great danger of forgetting God as the source of all. When this happens, we move into an idolatrous frame of mind. To see how this happens, we need to hear Athanasius at some length:

> For learning of the diverse forms of pleasure and girded with the forgetfulness of things divine, taking pleasure in the passions of the body and only in things of the moment, it paid regard to opinions about them and thought that nothing existed other than visible phenomena, and that only transitory

41. Athanasius, *On the Incarnation*, trans. a religious of CSMV (Crestwood, NY: St. Vladimir's Seminary Press, 1977), 44 (§16).

42. Ibid., 33 (§8).

> and bodily things were good. So perverted, and forgetting that it was made in the image of the good God, the soul no longer perceived through its own power God the Word, in whose form it had been created, but turning outside itself it regarded and pictured non-existent things. . . . It no longer saw what a soul should perceive, but, carried in every direction, it saw only what affected its senses. Hence, filled with every fleshly desire and confused by its notions of them, it then represented in bodily and tangible terms the God whom it had forgotten in its mind, applying the term "God" to visible phenomena and heeding only those things which it wished and regarded as pleasurable. The prime cause, therefore, of idolatry is evil.[43]

As Athanasius understands it, there is foolishness in the idolatrous gesture because it takes but a moment's reflection to see that one must be claiming to be a god in order to make a god, because the maker is always better than what he or she makes. That such god-makers die is proof enough that they are not gods. It would be more honest, though of course still silly, for the people who worship such idols to fix their gaze on the (mortal, fallible) idol maker.

But besides idolatry's foolishness, there is also the matter of its degrading all that comes within its sphere. Why? Because idolatry is the outgrowth of human passions that are irrational (Greek *alogos*). To fix our gaze, and thus also the ordering of our lives, on what is inherently irrational is to wreak havoc on the world. If Christ is the Word (*Logos*) that brings order, goodness, and beauty to the world, idolatry is the irrational, a-logical gesture that ends up undoing the world. Idolatry amounts to blindness, because idolaters can see only through the lens of their perverted hearts. "Just as those who turn away from the sun to dwell in the shade circle around in many pathless tracks, not seeing those at hand but imagining the absent to be present, and 'seeing do not see' [Matt. 13:13], in the same way those who have abandoned God and have darkened their souls have distracted minds, and like drunken and blind men they imagine things which don't exist."[44] Such people end up unleashing violence upon the world they profess to love because they love

43. Athanasius, *Contra Gentes*, ed. and trans. Robert W. Thomson (Oxford: Clarendon, 1971), 21 (§8).

44. Ibid., 65 (§23).

not what is but the phantasm they wish for. In other words, the idolatrous impulse distorts and harms creatures by causing us to see them in terms of the agendas that please us. They cannot be themselves because the idolater fails to see them in terms of the divine love that is constantly at work within them, leading them into the fullness of their life.

Creation means that the character and significance of the world become intelligible through the life of Jesus of Nazareth. His way of meeting, welcoming, nurturing, healing, reconciling, and celebrating others is the way of all created life at its best, because Christ's ways with creatures build and strengthen them to enter fully into the kinds of relationships that promote peace, resilience, and joy. As Graham Ward has put it, Christ is "the archetype of all relationship," meaning that in him we now see what every creaturely relationship should be.[45] Though creatures may for a time live within relationships that cause pain, alienation, and affliction, Jesus shows that this is not how relationships within creation are to be. Creation most becomes itself when it is healthy and whole, governed by peace and Sabbath delight. The seventh-century monk and theologian Maximus the Confessor gave powerful expression to this view when he wrote,

> The wisdom and sagacity of God the Father is the Lord Jesus Christ, who holds together the universals of beings by the power of wisdom, and embraces their complementary parts by the sagacity of understanding, since by nature he is the fashioner and provider of all, and through himself draws into one what is divided, and abolishes war between beings, and binds everything into peaceful friendship and undivided harmony.[46]

Christ is the eternal *Logos* who holds together all the *logoi* (words) that inform and direct created things to be what they are. Each thing in the world has a *logos* or principle of intelligibility and coherence within it that allows it to be the thing that it is. But creation as a whole is also directed in some way by principles of order and growth (otherwise it would have

45. Ward, *Christ and Culture*, 1.

46. Maximus the Confessor, *Ambigua* 41:1313B, in Andrew Louth, *Maximus the Confessor* (New York: Routledge, 1996), 161–62.

been impossible to call the world a *cosmos*) that enable mutual flourishing. Without the eternal *Logos* as the principle of loving harmony, what would hold the world together? Jesus the Word is intimately and personally present to each thing, leading it into the goodness and beauty of its own life but also of its life with others.

Put more generally, Jesus reveals the eternal Word to be the power of love at work within each thing and between all things, a power that leads and nurtures creation into fullness and life. Lossky makes the connection between each creaturely *logos* and the divine energies that express God's will for the world this way: "The divine 'willings' are the creative ideas of things, the *logoi*, the 'words.'. . . Every created thing has its point of contact with the Godhead; and this point of contact is the idea, reason or *logos* which is at the same time the end towards which it tends. . . . The whole is contained in the Logos, the second person of the Trinity who is the first principle and the last end of all created things."[47] Viewing the matter this way, we can see that it makes no sense at all to speak of "pure nature." Whatever is, is only because it already participates in the divine love that brings it into being, daily sustains it, and ultimately leads it to fulfillment in union with God. Creation is the good and beautiful place in which God's love is forever at work.

Put practically, Jesus shows us that the primary task of discipleship is for people to be a healing, nurturing, and reconciling presence in the world. When creatures are degraded, as they clearly are when animal livestock are kept in close, stifling confinement (all so that we can have cheap meat), or when mountains are blown to hell (all so that coal and electricity can be provided more cheaply), Christians are called to protest and protect the sanctity of life that is there under attack. They are called to implement and model ways of producing food and packaging energy that honor the goodness and beauty of creatures.[48] When this happens, Christians will in fact be "good news" to other creatures because they will be in the world in

47. Lossky, *Mystical Theology of the Eastern Church*, 98.

48. See my book (coauthored with Fred Bahnson) *Making Peace with the Land: God's Call to Reconcile with Creation* (Downers Grove, IL: InterVarsity, 2012) for examples of creation-honoring ways of food production. For further reading, see Jennifer Ayres, *Good Food: Grounded Practical Theology* (Waco: Baylor

ways that are sympathetic and harmonious. They will be ministers of a gospel that has been "proclaimed to every creature under heaven" (Col. 1:23).

Disciplined Perception

What remains for us to consider is how we today, living in a world marred by the effects of idolatry, can develop the perceptive capacities to see creation properly. How are our doors of perception to be cleansed so that when we see a creature we see it as the material manifestation of God's wisdom and love? What changes in the manner of our living need to occur before we can get into a position to apprehend what God wants us to sense?

In answering these questions we have much to learn from iconographic and monastic traditions, because they are so resolutely focused on the purification of perception. Recall that an icon is not about representing the world to us as it now is. It is, rather, about helping us see each thing in terms of its transfiguration in Christ. To see another as already participating in and enjoying God's loving presence requires that idolatrous ways of seeing that would reduce others to our desires and expectation have been overcome. For this reason Pavel Florensky argued that only saints can paint icons because they have undergone, and continue to undergo, a process of transformation in which, as Paul says in Galatians 2:20, it is no longer they who live but Christ who lives in and through them. The name for this kind of transformation is asceticism: "The ascetic purification of the soul, the removal from it of every subjective and accidental trace, reveals to the ascetic the rediscovered truth of human nature—the eternal truth of that creature created on the model of Christ, and therefore on *the absolute model*."[49] Throughout his writings Florensky maintained that the beauty of this world can be properly described only as God's love for the world. For us to see this beauty we must ourselves participate in this love. "In love and in love

University Press, 2013), and Mallory McDuff, *Natural Saints: How People of Faith Are Working to Save God's Earth* (New York: Oxford University Press, 2010).

49. Florensky, "On the Icon," 26.

alone is real knowledge of the Truth conceivable."[50] In other words, unless one undergoes the *metanoia* (Greek: change of heart and direction) and purification that make Christlike love effective in one's body and being, one will not be able to see another as God's creature.[51]

Asceticism is the path that leads us in this Christlike way. But asceticism, as reflected in various practices of renunciation like celibacy, fasting, and weeping, is often mischaracterized as hatred of the body and of material things. This is most unfortunate, because what asceticism is ultimately about is the correction of the chaotic desire and moral disorder within us so that we can perceive and welcome the world as God does. Asceticism is the discipline and art that, at its best, enables us to contemplate the beauty that radiates throughout creation. As such, asceticism is the prelude to true perception. Or as Florensky put it, "the aim to which the ascetic aspires is to perceive every creature in its first-created, victorious beauty. The Holy Spirit reveals Himself in the ability to see the beauty of creation. To always see the beauty in everything would mean 'to resurrect before the general resurrection' [Saint John Climacus], would mean to anticipate the final Revelation—the Comforter."[52]

Asceticism is the discipline that polishes the glass on our doors of perception so we can see the world as the manifestation of God's love, and then also go through the door to meet the world in acts of kindness, compassion, and hospitality. The action of loving, inspired as it is by the ministries of Christ, equips us to see the beauty of God at work in the world.[53]

50. Pavel Florensky, quoted in Victor Bychkov, *The Aesthetic Face of Being: Art in the Theology of Pavel Florensky* (Crestwood, NY: St. Vladimir's Seminary Press, 1993), 27.

51. Florensky developed this theme in *The Pillar and Ground of Truth: An Essay in Orthodox Theodicy in Twelve Letters* (Princeton: Princeton University Press, 2004), esp. "Letter Nine: Creation."

52. Ibid., 35–36. Christlike love so transforms persons that they can be said to have a different, new mind, what Paul in Phil. 2:5 and 1 Cor. 2:16 called "the mind of Christ."

53. Blowers provides the following helpful summary of Christ as the unifying, harmonizing *logos* of the world, who then serves as the pattern for our love in the world:

> Maximus' own admonition that the *logoi* of creation must be contemplated only through the focusing lens of the gospel of the crucified and risen Lord bespeaks the discipline of seeing the world as already shot through with

One's manner of approaching the world determines the kind of world one sees. Asceticism is all about attending to customary ways of approaching others that lead to distortion because what we see is dominated by the anxiety or hubris or insecurity we so often feel. Far too often we are blind to the fact that our attempts at loving are really masked forms of control or manipulation. Recognizing and healing this blindness is a necessary but difficult and long labor. To see how this is so, we turn now to monastic and contemplative traditions.

Learning to see others goes hand in hand with learning to see oneself. It is crucial to attend to oneself and to discover the deep currents that lead us to feel, think, and act in certain ways. When one begins this process, one quickly learns how much that motivates us functions in subterranean regions that elude conscious grasp. This means we are often not the best or most honest judges of ourselves. To understand ourselves we need the help of others to point out and bring to the surface the many impulses that promote the ego or that compel us to perceive things the way that we do. We need the discipline of Scripture reading and meditation to allow the Holy Spirit to read our lives. And we need regular and concentrated times of prayer to be quiet, to listen, and to attend to the many thoughts competing for control within us. The goal, as it often came to be summarized, is to learn to perceive in a dispassionate, detached manner.[54]

Maximus, who will serve as one of our guides in the exploration of contemplative perception, says, "A pure soul is one

the grace of the Creator's deep, kenotic condescension. Thus humanity does not look out upon the creation as "domain" per se but as the theatre of a cooperative mission with the triune Creator to lead creation toward its goal of reconciliation and transfiguration. . . . God calls humanity to exercise its freedom to cooperate with Christ in rebinding the particular and the universal in the grand network that is the cosmos. (*Drama of the Divine Economy*, 356–57)

54. Thomas Merton described this manner clearly in *New Seeds of Contemplation* (New York: New Directions, 1961) when he wrote, "We do not detach ourselves from things in order to attach ourselves to God, but rather we become detached *from ourselves* in order to see and use all things in and for God. . . . There is no evil in anything created by God, nor can anything of His become an obstacle to our union with Him. The obstacle is in our 'self,' that is to say in the tenacious need to maintain our separate, external, egotistic will" (21).

freed from passions and constantly delighted by divine love."[55] It is easy to misunderstand the meaning of the passions. When monks like Maximus decry the passions, they are not (in Stoic fashion) advocating a loveless or disengaged manner of life. They are instead concerned about how our attachments to others are saturated and distorted by anxiety, ambition, boredom . . . (the list goes on and on) so that authentic love for another becomes impossible. When we are filled with the passions, what we think is love for another turns out to be variations of love for oneself or love for the world as we desire it to be. Put in contemporary language, the passions lead us to want a world on our terms, on demand, and at a great price.

Dumitru Stăniloae, one of the great interpreters of Maximus in the twentieth century, said, "Passion is a knot of contradictions. It's the expression of an egotism which wants to make all things gravitate around it; it's the transformation of the world exclusively into a center of preoccupation as well. Passion is a product of the will of egocentric sovereignty; it's also a force which pushes man down to the state of an object carried here and there against his will. Sometimes it seeks the infinite; other times it chooses nothingness."[56] The contradictions at work are many, but one of the more glaring is readily to be seen in the kind of worship of the human body that ends up so objectifying it that it becomes degraded to the point of being fodder for the multibillion-dollar cosmetic, pornographic, and fashion industries. The body, we could say, falls within an idolatrous gaze that reduces it to an expendable toy or instrument.

At the heart of the passions we often find the belief that the self is an autonomous, independent absolute. As Maximus puts it, self-love is the mother of the passions. This means that we go to great lengths to satisfy ourselves and bring glory to ourselves. Self-love leads to deep forms of attachment that actually get in the way of a welcoming and open embrace of another. Self-love makes harmony with each other and the world a virtual impossibility.

55. Maximus the Confessor, *Four Hundred Texts on Love*, in *The Philokalia*, vol. 2, trans. G. E. H. Palmer, Philip Sherrard, and Kallistos Ware (London: Faber & Faber, 1981), 56 (1.34).

56. Dumitru Stăniloae, *Orthodox Spirituality* (South Canaan, PA: St. Tikhon's Seminary Press, 2003), 79.

Monastic detachment, we can now see, is not detachment from the world, as if created things were somehow evil, but rather detachment from oneself and from the deep desires that get in the way of welcoming others for who or what they are. For Maximus, the creatures of this world are not evil. They could not be, because they are the work of God. That means that the problem is not the world but the disordered faculties within ourselves that prevent us from perceiving and engaging the world in an open, truthful, and compassionate manner.

Among the faculties one of the most important is clearly the heart, the deep center within ourselves that prompts us to desire and do things in the world. But another crucial faculty is the intellect, the power within us that enables us to see and then characterize things as being this or that kind of thing. How we name and narrate the world is important because it is our naming and narrating that determine how we will relate to it. "Things are outside the intellect, but the conceptual images of these things are formed within it. It is consequently in the intellect's power to make good or bad use of these conceptual images. Their wrong use is followed by the misuse of the things themselves."[57] It is thus of the highest importance that the intellect be trained to watch for how the passions infiltrate and distort the conceptual images we make of things. "The intellect functions in accordance with nature when it keeps the passions under control, contemplates the inner essences of created beings, and abides with God."[58]

This brief look at how the passions distort our seeing and knowing of the world enables us to make some crucial observations about what it means to see creation. Such seeing begins with attention to how personal ambition, fear, and boredom get in the way of seeing things for what they are, that is, expressions of God's love, and as such, the material manifestations of God's goodness and delight. "God, full beyond all fullness, brought creatures into being not because He had need of anything, but so that they might participate in Him in proportion to their capacity and that He Himself might rejoice in His works (cf. Ps. 104:31), through seeing them joyful and ever filled to overflowing with His inexhaustible gifts."[59]

57. Maximus the Confessor, *Four Hundred Texts on Love*, 77 (2.73).
58. Ibid., 105 (4.45).
59. Ibid., 90 (3.56).

Attentive self-regard, informed by the reading of the Scriptures and corrected by the promptings of the Holy Spirit, leads next to the cleansing of our perceptive and cognitive faculties so that we can approach others without the many, sometimes conflicting, agendas we bring into the world. Only then can genuine love of others take root in us. Only then can our love be said to be a witness to and participation in the selfless, Christlike love that gives life to the world in gestures of healing, nurture, reconciliation, and celebration. In this love the other is not absorbed into me or made to somehow satisfy aims that I have chosen. It is, rather, a hospitable love in which my attention and energy circulate around the other in seeking the other's well-being. To see creation means that we need, in ecstatic fashion, to go out from ourselves to meet others on their own terms. This ecstatic movement is the movement of self-offering love.

Self-offering love is a practical skill rather than merely a pious sentiment. To practice it, disciples need to learn the arts of neighborliness, arts like home construction, food production, machine invention and repair, medicine and health care, town planning and design, and education—all done with the clear purpose of enabling others to maximally develop their own lives and our shared life together. In certain respects, this will require a fairly radical re-visioning of forms of Christianity that have focused on individual "spiritual" attainment at the expense of "right livelihood" and a just economy. As Berry put it, "You cannot know that life is holy if you are content to live from economic practices that daily destroy life and diminish its possibility."[60]

Is perceiving creation the ultimate goal? Depending on the monastic text or author one reads, one might think that our final goal is to leave creation altogether behind so that we can attain something like a pure vision of God. In Maximus, for instance, we read, "Love is the holy state of the soul, disposing it to value knowledge of God above all created things. We cannot attain lasting possession of such love while we are still attached to anything worldly."[61] Or, "It is said that the highest state of prayer is reached when the intellect goes beyond the

60. Wendell Berry, "Christianity and the Survival of Creation," in *Art of the Commonplace*, 309.

61. Maximus the Confessor, *Four Hundred Texts on Love*, 53 (1.1).

flesh and the world, and while praying is utterly free from matter and form. He who maintains this state has truly attained unceasing prayer."[62] Maximus is not alone in warning of the dangers of attachments to a world that is transitory, ephemeral, and the source of so much pain and heartache. But is this way of speaking a reflection of residual dualism, or a sneaking-in of gnostic impulses, and thus fundamentally a denial of God's love made real in a material world?

The difficulty is how to balance an affirmation of the goodness of creation with the long histories of idolatrous appropriation of it. The crucial insight to remember is that a Christian perception of the world is, as Saint Isaac the Syrian said, "the experience of all things in God," which means that right perception will always, at the same time, draw us more closely into a recognition of and participation in the love of God. What needs emphasis is that every creature is what it is only because God loves and sustains it in its being. Each created thing is the material manifestation of God's love—what the Orthodox tradition calls God's "energies"—at work within it. To reject any such creature would thus amount to a rejection of God's love. If the created world is a participation in God's life—as Maximus puts it, each creaturely *logos* is embraced by the eternal, divine *Logos* (without the *Logos* being contained within any creature)[63]—it would seem that any form of disparagement or abandonment of creation amounts to a denial of God. Or as we saw when attending to iconographic traditions in theology, the disparagement of matter is ultimately a disparagement of the incarnation.

The call to leave the world of matter behind or to transcend its materiality is a dangerous call if it leads people to a denial of God's creative love in the world. Why? Because such denial inevitably leads to the world's degradation and destruction rather than its healing and redemption. A better way to proceed is to live with the warning about the difficulty of appreciating how passions and attachments intervene in even our best efforts to cleanse our souls and participate in the ways of love. Douglas Christie has recently pointed out that when a person is deeply devoted and open to a loving reception of the world,

62. Ibid., 76 (2.61).

63. Maximus the Confessor, *Two Hundred Texts on Theology*, in *The Philokalia*, vol. 2, 139–40 (2.10).

it is but a matter of time before that person realizes that no image, no thought, no word can be fully faithful to what is seen and engaged. We saw this at the start of this chapter when we witnessed the difficulty Cézanne and Oliver had in representing the world adequately. Our temptation, perhaps even our default setting, to use the language of Marion, would be to halt an infinite gaze at some finite, manageable point, and thus render the gaze idolatrous.

Reflecting on artistic attempts to come to terms with the endlessness and mystery of the world around him, Christie notes that becoming clear-sighted is an infinite journey into depth. Cézanne, like other painters, admitted that he was "becoming more aware of [the world's] endless complexity and intricacy, the shifting moods of a place depending on the time of day and season. It cannot be grasped or known, not completely. It can only be seen, partially and provisionally. Then seen again. And yet again. Here one senses the recognition of the need for a kind of *rumination* in which one can be drawn ever deeper into the mystery of what one beholds, and forward in search of the forms that can best express what one sees."[64]

Seen with these concerns in mind, perhaps the call to leave all images behind should be interpreted not as an abandonment of the world but as an abandonment of the fixity or finality of any image *for the sake of a deeper and more sympathetic engagement with the freshness, surprise, and mystery of creation.* There is, in other words, an indispensable apophatic dimension to all perception of creation, a dimension in which quiet and silence and the acknowledgment of our ignorance are allowed to chasten personal desire and ambition. Such an interpretation, I think, would speak well to our faltering, too often destructive attempts to live faithfully in a world of God's inexhaustible love. It would speak to the unfathomable grace that circulates throughout creation and that calls us to perceive in the first place. And it would create in us the humility and the openness that are prerequisite for us becoming available to address the needs and the potential of fellow creatures.

64. Christie, *Blue Sapphire of the Mind*, 173 (emphasis original).

4

The Human Art of Creaturely Life

> There appears to be a law that when creatures have reached the level of consciousness, as men have, they must become conscious of the creation; they must learn how they fit into it and what its needs are and what it requires of them, or else pay a terrible penalty: the spirit of the creation will go out of them, and they will become destructive; the very earth will depart from them and go where they cannot follow.
>
> Wendell Berry, "A Native Hill"

> Human beings have lost their creaturely nature; this has been corrupted by their being *sicut deus* [like god]. The whole created world is now covered in a veil; it is silent and lacking explanation, opaque and enigmatic.
>
> Dietrich Bonhoeffer, *Creation and Fall*

In 1988 Jean-Luc Nancy convened a group of leading French philosophers to consider the question, "Who comes after the Subject?" Nancy wanted to assess the status of human subjectivity after considerable reflection upon it by thinkers as diverse as Hegel, Marx, Nietzsche, Freud, Heidegger, Bataille, and Wittgenstein, but he also wanted to explore what such reflection looks like in the wake of a century punctuated by war, fascism, the gulag, technophilia, environmental degradation, and the development of economic imperialism. Far from being a nihilistic exercise in the obliteration of subjectivity or the self, this endeavor was Nancy's attempt to see how our thinking about subjectivity might be opened up to fresh thoughts and new possibilities. Given numerous philosophical critiques, and a century in which "civilized" people committed acts of unspeakable horror, there could be no simple "return to the subject." We need to move forward to someone. But to *whom*? The question was how to name, narrate, and receive this "someone."

As we have already seen, modernity gave birth to forms of subjectivity in which human beings are the source and the center of value. Modernity established subjects as autonomous beings, as those who give the moral law to themselves, but it also declared human beings as the ones who determine the measures by which everything is to be sorted and weighed. I described this development as the outworking of an idolatrous impulse because modern subjectivity results in the remaking of the world in ways that bring satisfaction and glory to us. No longer content to contemplate the world so as to determine how humanity might fit harmoniously within the orders of reality, people, armed with the powers of new technologies, now set out to engineer the world in their own image. By the twentieth century's end it had become clear—in the lives and lands wasted and destroyed—that this experiment in engineering the world led to the twin disasters of genocide and ecocide. Therefore, we need to consider what sort of *being* is the human being who brings nurture and healing, rather than degradation and destruction, to the world.

In this chapter I argue that, from a Christian point of view, it is *creatureliness* that comes after (and before) the subject. I maintain that creatureliness is a more faithful and compelling rendition of human life than are modern characterizations of subjectivity that have often been uncritically absorbed by Christians. Creatureliness is the overarching metaphysical framework in terms of which human life and action receive their significance and value. My fundamental presupposition is that creatureliness goes to the heart of human identity and vocation, illuminating both *who* we are and *what we are to do*.

What it means to name and narrate human life in terms of its creatureliness, however, is anything but simple. In part this is because theologians have often missed opportunities to develop the anthropological insights found in the doctrine of creation.[1] "Creatureliness" is not an established theological category that shows up in seminary syllabi or in Sunday school curricula. Moreover, it is also the case that humanity's sinful condition—what Dietrich Bonhoeffer described as our striving to become like god (*sicut deus*)—marks an abiding rebellion against creatureliness.[2] In other words, people don't want to be creatures. They want to be exceptional, or, more precisely, they wish to be exempt from the challenges and responsibilities that follow from a creaturely condition.

My account of creatureliness will begin by developing an agrarian picture of creaturely identity by engaging several key elements of Genesis 2–3, the oldest creation story in Scripture. As I develop this account, I will appropriate Bonhoeffer's suggestive theological commentary on this passage that he presented at the University of Berlin in the 1932–33 winter course Creation and Sin. I will also put this commentary in conversation with writers who have been critical of the construct called "the modern subject," all with the aim of opening a space for

1. David Kelsey's magisterial two-volume *Eccentric Existence: A Theological Anthropology* (Louisville: Westminster John Knox, 2009) is a notable exception to this tendency. Kelsey observes, along with Gustaf Wingren, that the doctrine of creation does "remarkably little work" in modern systematic theology (160). Admittedly, a considerable amount has been written about humanity made in the image of God (*imago Dei*). What is striking about many of these accounts, however, is how much they rely on philosophical characterizations of capacities such as reason or language or the soul that do not have their inspiration in biblical depictions of creation and creatureliness. For a lucid treatment showing why these accounts are theologically unsatisfactory, see Ian McFarland's *The Divine Image: Envisioning the Invisible God* (Minneapolis: Fortress, 2005).

2. Speaking of sin, Bonhoeffer observes, "The word *disobedience* fails to describe the situation adequately. It is rebellion, the creature's stepping outside of the creature's only possible attitude, the creature's becoming creator, the destruction of creatureliness, a defection, a falling away [*Sturzen*] from being safely held as a creature" (*Creation and Fall* [Minneapolis: Fortress, 1997], 120 [hereafter cited in text as *CF*]).

a reconsideration of persons *as* creatures. I will conclude by showing how a recovery of the human art of creaturely life is made real and practical in the ways we grow food and eat with each other.

Our Garden Context

It is of profound theological and anthropological significance that the earliest biblical creation story places human beings in a garden. Why this agrarian setting as opposed to some other? Bonhoeffer suggested the setting represented a fantasy: for the Israelites, living as they did in an arid region and on marginal land, what could be more magnificent than a garden with rich soil, abundant water, and trees laden with beautiful and delectable fruit? This is why he argued that the garden imagery of this story needed to be translated into the language of today's technical world (*CF*, 81–83).

We should ask if Bonhoeffer's judgment is not itself a reflection of a modern, urban forgetfulness of and bias against agrarian ways of understanding human identity and life, ways that were common to most of humanity in the last ten thousand years, and that were presupposed by the writers and hearers of Scripture.[3] Is not the rebellion against creatureliness that Bonhoeffer powerfully describes mirrored in humanity's long-standing rebellion against the land? Perhaps the agrarian, garden setting, along with the practical sympathies and sensibilities it makes possible, is crucial because of its unique ability to illuminate our condition.

I should be clear at the start that my advocacy for agrarian sensitivities and responsibilities is not a recommendation that all people be farmers or professional gardeners. Owing to the complex intelligence and diverse skill set required, and the practical, logistical problems associated with moving a large population "back to the land," relatively few people are cut out for this kind of work. What I am arguing is that all people, no matter their location and occupation, must appreciate the

3. Ellen Davis has developed the agrarian context for understanding Israelite history and its theological traditions in *Scripture, Culture, and Agriculture: An Agrarian Reading of the Bible* (New York: Cambridge University Press, 2009).

fundamental importance of the land as the source and destination of their life, and therefore also make an encompassing, practical commitment to implement and support economies that promote the health of people and land *together*. This is no small matter, especially if we acknowledge that throughout much of history, economic "success" has been at the expense of, and has exhausted, the land.[4]

Agrarian sympathies are crucial because without them people run the risk of distorting the character of their lives. Working with the land, people come to understand the importance of the practices of attention and care, seeing that without a commitment to care for the soil and all its creatures, the prospect of a flourishing human life comes to an end. This is why in agrarian cultures people's desires and expectations are calibrated to meet the needs of the land. There can be no healthy people without a healthy land to feed them and provide for their needs.

To commit to learn to care is not easy because it is accompanied by a sobering realization: "Care is constantly being thrown back upon the limitations of its powers of action, is constantly reminded of its own inefficacy and essential passivity when it comes to phenomena like weather, blight, parasites, and rodents."[5] To farm or garden is to become acquainted with amazement and bewilderment in the presence of the world. But it is also to have to face human ignorance and impotence—there is so much we don't understand, and the powers we bring to the world are so often misapplied.

More deeply, in the work of nurturing plant and animal life, people come into intimate contact with the powers of death as the matrix in terms of which life's potential unfolds. Gardens are places where people learn that death is not simply an end to life, but a vital ingredient and partner in the furthering of life. Put simply, there is no fertility without the deaths of countless bodies entering the ground. It is a humbling, even terrifying, thing to

4. For a lucid description of how the unmooring of economy from ecology leads to the collapse of civilizations, see David R. Montgomery, *Dirt: The Erosion of Civilizations* (Berkeley: University of California Press, 2007), and James Gustave Speth, *The Bridge at the Edge of the World: Capitalism, the Environment, and Crossing from Crisis to Sustainability* (New Haven: Yale University Press, 2008).

5. Robert Pogue Harrison, *Gardens: An Essay on the Human Condition* (Chicago: University of Chicago Press, 2008), 28.

acknowledge one's dependence on the deaths of others. To be entirely removed from the places of agrarian work, and to be oblivious to or even despise agrarian sympathies and practices—a condition that is very much the norm in today's urban and suburban contexts—is, therefore, to run the risk of being naïve about, and therefore also irresponsible with, human life.

Noted African American author bell hooks has observed that when people lose a practical, working connection with the land, they risk becoming dysfunctional at their core. This is because a full affirmation of human dignity presupposes respect for human bodies *and* the land in terms of which these bodies are fed and clothed and warmed. Reflecting on the history of her own people, hooks argues that as long as black folks lived close to nature, growing food and flowers, they remained close to life-creating processes that did not discriminate among people. One could say, they remained close to and felt affirmed by the divine power at work in the world.

Respect for human bodies and respect for lands go together and are intimately tied to the understanding that soil and the many processes of life and death are sacred. To despise the work that nurtures and protects the land, by consigning it to slave labor, for instance, is ultimately also to despise the bodies that draw their livelihood from the land.

> To tend the earth is always then to tend our destiny, our freedom and our hope. . . . To live in communion with the earth, fully acknowledging nature's power with humility and grace, is a practice of spiritual mindfulness that heals and restores. Making peace with the earth we make the world a place where we can be one with nature. We create and sustain environments where we can come back to ourselves, where we can return home, stand on solid ground, and be a true witness.[6]

One cannot degrade land without also degrading human bodies, because it is only in terms of the health of the former that the well-being of the latter can be sought.

Slavery was clearly a profound disrespecting of black bodies. What is not so clearly appreciated is that the nineteenth-century

6. bell hooks, *Belonging: A Culture of Place* (New York: Routledge, 2009), 117, 119–20.

removal of black folks from the land played a major role in the degradation of black culture. As long as African Americans farmed land, they knew that their life flowed from the powers of the soil and the fertility of plants, rather than the unjust laws of white culture. Though whites might claim to dominate black bodies, they could not dominate the body of the earth. "When black people migrated to urban cities, this humanizing connection with nature was severed; racism and white supremacy came to be seen as all powerful, the ultimate factors informing our fate. When this thinking was coupled with a breakdown in religiosity, a refusal to recognize the sacred in everyday life, it served the interests of white supremacist capitalist patriarchy."[7] For hooks, agrarian ways and sensitivities are crucial lest we lose sight of the land as the source of our nurture, freedom, and hope. When black people lost their empowering connection with the land—both through slavery and then through urbanization—they lost more than a way of life. To forget one's grounding in the soil is to become spiritually adrift and confused. It is to forget that one's value is affirmed fundamentally in the divine gift of land and bodies that are daily nurtured by God, and is not dependent on the valuations of imperialist cultures that seek to control bodies to their own ends.

What, then, does the garden scene in Genesis 2, particularly its reference to the creation of the first human being (*'adam*), formed out of fertile soil (*'adamah*), say about creaturely life? Most basically, it says that creatureliness is inescapably marked by need and by dependence on fellow creatures and a creator. It is easy to overlook the significance of what is being communicated here: the need and dependence that mark human life, though clearly having social and political dimensions, are first and forever experienced in bodily attachments to sun and plants, soil and butterflies that are unavoidable because it is *through* them—most basically in the form of eating—that we live at all.

Genesis 2 describes human life, but also plant (2:9) and animal (2:19) life, as fundamentally and inextricably bound to and

7. Ibid., 118. Hooks advises, "More than ever before in our nation's history, black folks must collectively renew our relationship to the earth, to our agrarian roots. For when we are forgetful and participate in the destruction and exploitation of dark earth, we collude with the domination of the earth's dark bodies, both here and globally" (119).

dependent upon soil. Soil is the recombinant and regenerative matrix out of which all terrestrial life comes, and to which it eventually returns. As Wendell Berry puts it, "The soil is the great connector of lives, the source and destination of all. It is the healer and restorer and resurrector, by which disease passes into health, age into youth, death into life. Without proper care for it we can have no community, because without proper care for it we can have no life."[8] To rebel against soil—as when we poison or erode it—or even to neglect it, is to take a stance against creation.

Genesis 2 further shows creaturely life as ultimately dependent on God's life-giving creativity, creativity that takes an intensely intimate form: God's own breath as the power of life within our own, lifting soil to an animated and *adamic* form.[9] Soil is never simply dirt or dirty. It is the bearer of the divine breath of life.[10] Creaturely life is possible only because, as David Kelsey says in *Eccentric Existence*, it breathes a "borrowed breath" from God. According to the psalmist, the day God withholds this divine breath is also the day creatures die and return to lifeless dust (*'aphar*). But:

> When you send forth your spirit [breath, *ruakh*], they are created;
> and you renew the face of the ground [*'adamah*].
> (Ps. 104:30)

8. Wendell Berry, *The Unsettling of America: Culture and Agriculture* (San Francisco: Sierra Club Books, 1977), 86.

9. Scripture leaves it open as to whether or not the divine breath that animates the *'adam* also animates plant and animal life. The King James Version made a clear distinction between human and nonhuman creaturely life by saying the former became a "living soul," whereas the animals were "living creatures." The Hebrew, however, does not allow this neat (and entirely advantageous to us) bifurcation, since it names humans *and* animals as *nefesh hayah*.

10. In his autobiographical essay "A Native Hill" (in *The Long-Legged House* [1969; repr., Washington, DC: Shoemaker & Hoard, 2004]), Berry says,

> The most exemplary nature is that of the topsoil. It is very Christ-like in its passivity and beneficence, and in the penetrating energy that issues out of its peaceableness. It increases by experience, by the passage of seasons over it, growth arising out of it and returning to it, not by ambition or aggressiveness. It is enriched by all things that die and enter into it. It keeps the past, not as history or as memory, but as richness, new possibility. Its fertility is always building up out of death into promise. Death is the bridge or the tunnel by which its past enters its future. (204)

It is an astounding thing to say that the life of God begins and finds a basic (and abiding) point of contact in the ground beneath our feet. Owing to various forms of dualism that elevate the soul above the body, and spiritual reality above the material realm, Christians have been taught to "look up" for a God somewhere beyond the blue. Scripture does not support an exclusive upward focus. God is to be met in the most intimate and practical places of our lives as the source of life's inspiration and nurture, which also means that God's love is to be encountered in such mundane places as our physical need for food, warmth, health, and companionable touch. The place of God is the place of the whole creature's need and fulfillment.

The dependence described in the Genesis story is not abstract or optional. It is embodied, and smelt in every breath and tasted in every swallow and bite. Appreciating it presupposes active engagement and skilled work. This is why God enlists the human creature to till and keep the garden (Gen. 2:15), because it is through the tending and serving of fellow creatures that the *'adam* practically probes and potentially learns to appreciate the range, depth, and responsibilities of interdependent life.[11] Without the gardening work that leads us more deeply and sympathetically into the complexities and mysteries of soil, people are prone to become naïve and negligent. According to this story, it is crucial we keep our hands familiar with soil so that we don't forget our need and dependence, but also our responsibility to care for the bodies

11. The NRSV translation of Genesis 2:15 as "till and keep" clearly resonates with the horticultural context of this passage. Davis argues that the root verb "to work or till" can have a variety of meanings ranging from working the land to working *for* the land (as a form of service to it, and perhaps even worship to God). The verb "to keep" also has the meaning "to observe" (as when the Israelites are told to observe God's commandments), suggesting that "keeping" presupposes personal alignment or attunement to what is going on and expected in the garden. Davis suggests the translation, "And YHWH God took the human and set him in the garden of Eden to work and serve it, to preserve and observe it" (*Scripture, Culture, and Agriculture*, 30). This translation highlights how the *'adam* needs to develop the very practical skills of attention, patient work, and respect for limits and possibilities. The human creature must show humility as one who draws its life from humus. I have developed the meaning of humility in "The Touch of Humility: An Invitation to Creatureliness," in *Modern Theology* 24, no. 2 (April 2008): 225–44.

we live through. Gardening work—all the attention, patience, and skill it requires—is the fundamental entry point and training ground for the practices of care that mark humanity's creaturely condition.

Human creaturely identity and vocation come together in the work of gardening, work that is foundational rather than optional. This work is not the reflection of a curse. It couldn't be, because God is the Essential Gardener, the one who relates to the world in modes of intimacy, protection, and delight. Moreover, given that God is cast as the First Gardener (Gen. 2:8), we are led to think that human participation in the work of gardening is also a growing in our understanding of God's creative, attentive, patient, and nurturing ways. It is a striking thing to say, as this story does, that God relates to the world as a gardener to his or her garden. What it means is that people, insofar as they aspire to live into the image and likeness of God, must take up the disciplines of care and celebration that are at the heart of all good gardening work. Gardening, in short, is the complex activity that leads us into a deeper encounter with and understanding of creation, creatureliness, and the Creator's life.

My interpretation of Genesis presupposes an appreciation for how gardens are indispensable places in which insights about creatureliness can be learned.[12] Here, amidst water, soil, plant, animal, weather, and sun, gardeners work to understand as precisely as possible the character of the relationships and responsibilities that make eating and drinking, and therefore

12. It is important to underscore that gardens are built environments to the extent that they are the coming together of wild/natural forces with human design and skill. But unlike other built environments (a shopping mall, for instance), in which *human* ingenuity, technology, and ambition dominate and are continually reflected back to us, gardens are places in which people are more readily compelled to see the variety and complexity of creatures and life processes *beyond* human design or control. The philosopher David Copper describes the deep meaning and attraction of gardens as residing, in part, in their ability to reveal "the relation between the source of the world and ourselves" (*A Philosophy of Gardens* [Oxford: Clarendon, 2006], 150). Speaking of the great variety of gardening traditions around the world, he stresses that attention to the "source of the world" brings us face-to-face with the mystery of things as present and somehow given. "The Garden, to put it portentously, is an epiphany of man's relationship to mystery. This relationship is its mystery" (145).

also the many quotidian elements of our life together, possible. Here people discover that the sources of health and vitality are never simply "resources" awaiting our procurement, but are instead the fruit of a mysterious, fresh, enlivening power that transforms death into fertility and seed into fruit.[13] In gardens life is daily witnessed and felt to be vulnerable and fragile, but also surprising and miraculous. Here people learn that life's celebration is necessarily accompanied, and made more honest, by life's care. We become good gardeners insofar as we learn to work with the powers of life that exceed our comprehension and control, even as we engage them to meet our needs. If we are attentive, we will clearly see how easy it is for human agency to destroy the sources of life.

As those who work closely with soil can testify, the power of life witnessed in gardens is a "dark" power because it so often leaves gardeners in varying states of incomprehension. Gardens are places of inexplicable fecundity and freshness, but also disease and death. Here human ingenuity and ambition are frequently revealed as floundering, contentious movements that lead to failure rather than fruit. Gardening

13. The poet Rainer Maria Rilke (1875–1926) writes in Sonnet 12 of *The Sonnets to Orpheus: First Series*, in *Duino Elegies and the Sonnets to Orpheus*, trans. A. Poulin Jr. (New York: Mariner, 2005), 107:

> Though he works and worries, the farmer
> never reaches down to where the seed turns
> into summer. The earth *grants*.

Wendell Berry speaks similarly in a Sabbath poem from *A Timbered Choir: The Sabbath Poems, 1979-1997* (Washington, DC: Counterpoint, 1998), 18 (reproduced with permission):

> Whatever is foreseen in joy
> Must be lived out from day to day.
> Vision held open in the dark
> By our ten thousand days of work.
> Harvest will fill the barn; for that
> The hand must ache, the face must sweat.
>
> And yet no leaf or grain is filled
> By work of ours; the field is tilled
> And left to grace. That we may reap,
> Great work is done while we're asleep.

is a form of work that perpetually undoes our knowing and unseats the gardener as the center of primary significance. It demands forms of attention, patience, and humility that, for good reason, parallel the ascetic movements of mystical quests.[14] Gardening is a form of asceticism because it shows us how much we are inclined to install ourselves at the center of the universe, and thus forget that the welcome and nurture of others requires us to engage them on their terms. Berry puts it this way:

> Until we understand what the land is, we are at odds with everything we touch. And to come to that understanding it is necessary, even now, to leave the regions of our conquest—the cleared fields, the towns and cities, the highways—and re-enter the woods. For only there can man encounter the silence and darkness of his own absence. Only in this silence and darkness can he recover the sense of the world's longevity, of its ability to thrive without him, of his inferiority to it and his dependence on it. Perhaps then, having heard that silence and seen that darkness, he will grow humble before the place and begin to take it in—to learn *from it* what it is. As its sounds come into his hearing, and its lights and colors come into his vision, and its odors come into his nostrils, then he may come into *its* presence as he never has before, and he will arrive in his place and will want to remain. His life will grow out of the ground like the other lives of the place, and take its place among them. He will be *with* them—neither ignorant of them, nor indifferent to them, nor against them—and so at last he will grow to be native-born. That is, he must re-enter the silence and darkness, and be born again.[15]

To enter into the knowledge of their own creatureliness, people must live and work with the dark, that is, with an honest appreciation of their ignorance and impotence. They must learn to calm the ravenous and rapacious intellect that wants, through its knowing, to comprehend and control the world. It is through darkness that the creative light that nourishes the

14. I have developed this theme in "The Dark Night of the Soil: An Agrarian Approach to Mystical Life," in *Christianity and Literature* 56, no. 2 (Winter 2007): 253–74.

15. Berry, "A Native Hill," 207.

world can be beheld. It is in the quiet that another can finally be heard.[16]

When the Genesis 2 story is read through an agrarian lens, it becomes apparent that Scripture understands human life as finite, bound, and limited. Our dependence on the Creator and on fellow creatures means that life is never our own (as a possession) or within our conceptual grasp (as a manageable object). Who we *are*, our ontological status, is to be *in need* of and *in relationship* with a bewildering array of others, constantly receiving from them the many forms of bodily nurture and imaginative inspiration that make everyday life possible. Nothing is more indicative of this fact than our daily need to breathe, drink, and eat. To be a creature is, therefore, to be incomplete, in-breathed, un-self-sufficient, and unable to rise and stand on one's own. Human identity is open, varied, and unfinished because it is always being worked out with the creatures we meet and the relationships we live through.

My interpretation of Genesis 2 shows that creatureliness means that we are always already, and viscerally (through lungs and stomachs), implicated in and in-formed by others—bacteria, worms, butterflies, chickens, cows, gardeners—all of which together depend on the wild power of God as their source. Though creatures can be centers of agency in their own unique ways, nevertheless God is intimately and mysteriously present in the liveliness witnessed in their activity. Creaturely life is always life *received* from God and *inspired* and *nurtured* by others. To "be" is to be dependent and vulnerable, daily faced with the incomprehensibility of ourselves and the world in which we move. It is to be marked by potential, but also always by *need*, and therefore also *responsibility* for and *gratitude* to others.

16. O bent by fear and sorrow, now bend down,

Leave word and argument, be dark and still,
And come into the joy of healing shade.
Rest from your work. Be still and dark until

You grow as unopposing, unafraid
As the young trees, without thought or belief;
Until the shadow Sabbath light has made

Shudders, breaks open, shines in every leaf.
(Berry, *Timbered Choir*, 31;
reproduced with permission)

Refusing Creatureliness

Bonhoeffer's commentary on Genesis 2, though not focused on the agrarian dimensions I have outlined, is important because it developed an understanding of creatureliness centered on need, finitude, and limit. Referring to the placement of the tree of life *and* the tree of the knowledge of good and evil at the garden's center, he observed, "*The human being's limit is at the center of human existence*, not on the margin. . . . The boundary that is at the center is the limit of human *reality*, of human *existence as such*" (*CF*, 86; emphasis original). In other words, a limit is not an obstacle or challenge that lies before us as something to be overcome and then left behind. If it were, it would be at the periphery of our lives as the domain *not yet* appropriated and internalized.

Theologically understood, limit goes to the core of our being because it marks us as ones who must constantly go to the tree of life and receive life as a gift from *beyond* our own power. Ecologically understood, limit describes our condition as embodied creatures that daily draw on ecosystems and ecosystem processes for life. Limit encompasses the whole of being and every possible disposition and manifestation of human life. This is why Bonhoeffer argued that Adam recognizes and realizes himself not by overcoming the limit but by embracing and gratefully receiving it as the blessing that animates and nurtures him through life. "Adam does not know the boundary as something that can be transgressed; otherwise Adam would know about evil. Adam knows it as the given grace that belongs to his creatureliness and freedom. Adam also knows, therefore, that life is possible only because of the limit" (*CF*, 87).

According to Bonhoeffer's interpretation of this story, it is crucial to understand that limit and need are perceived by Adam not as deficiency but as good because Adam thereby acknowledges that he lives by grace rather than through the power of his own might. Here we come to a crucial insight about creaturely life: the acknowledgment of creatureliness goes hand in hand with the disposition to gratefully receive life as a gift from God. "The limit is grace because it is the basis of creatureliness and freedom; the boundary is the center. Grace is that which holds humankind over the abyss of nonbeing, nonliving, not-being-created" (*CF*, 87). The prohibition against eating from the tree of the knowledge of good and evil is not at first a temptation. As far as Adam is concerned, the prohibition pertaining to this particular tree is part of the grace of creaturely life that is already understood to be marked and enlivened by limit.

As is well known, Adam and Eve transgress the limit.[17] They appropriate and internalize it in a most graphic way: by eating. In this eating they precipitated death, for as God had said earlier to Adam, "for in the day that you eat of it [the tree of the knowledge of good and evil] you shall die" (2:17). What does this "death" mean, particularly if we understand that creaturely life—granted as a gift rather than grasped as a possession—was marked by mortality from the beginning? Bonhoeffer is clear that the death spoken about by God is not cessation of biological existence. Instead it is a dishonest and damaging way of existing. It is dishonest because it denies that we daily depend on others and upon God for life. It is damaging because it transforms a world of grace into an arena of competitive grasping and self-glorifying manipulation, what we earlier described as a place for the exercise of multiple idolatries.

Genuine, creaturely life is marked by the humble, grateful reception of life as a gracious gift from God, and is witnessed in the responsible care of fellow creatures. Deathly "life," the existence that disrespects and violates limits, is marked by the obligation to live from *out of oneself*, and is witnessed in the exploitation of others (others are seen to matter to the extent that they can support one's living out of oneself). But this is an impossible, frustrating obligation, and a fundamental self-deception, because no creature is the source of its own life. Wanting to live from and in terms set by itself, the self eventually recognizes—the moment it eats!—that it depends on others.

17. Bonhoeffer proposes that prior to the transgression, Adam lived in respectful obedience to the grace of life. His obedience made possible a unified, singularly focused form of life in which the two-sidedness of good and evil, i.e., the prospect of an option that diverges from obedience, had not yet emerged. The possibility of good versus evil, therefore, only emerges *in* the transgressive act. This is why Bonhoeffer thinks Adam first lives "beyond good and evil" (*CF*, 87). The option is not between good and evil but between a "life obedient to God" and "a life of good and evil."

In the frustration of knowing that we cannot live from out of ourselves and on terms set entirely by us, rebellion against our creaturely condition is born. Rebellion is not confined to the personal realm. It moves through the world like ripples across a pond, and results in the degradation and death of others as their integrity and sanctity are denied so that they can serve a self-satisfying end. In the effort to secure life and make it susceptible to his decision, Adam puts himself in opposition to the animation and nurture of God. He is unable to acknowledge and appropriately respect his life as lived *from*, *with*, and *through* others, nor is he able to affirm and receive others as gifts of God. Adam refuses grace, denies his life as a blessing, but must continue on as one defined by need.

The death Adam introduces into the world is not biological death. It is something like an existential condition that means "no longer being able to live before God, and yet having to live before God. It means standing before God as an outlaw, as one who is lost and damned, but not as one who no longer exists" (*CF*, 90). In seeking to secure life on his own terms, and by trying to live from out of himself, Adam shows his rebellion against creatureliness and the Creator. He sets in motion a history of humanity that is set *against* limit. As Bonhoeffer understands it, it is the human rebellion against, and refusal of, our creaturely condition that leads to the degradation of the world.

It would be an enormously complex task to demonstrate the many ways in which modern characterizations of the subject represent the fulfillment of this rebellious spirit.[18] What is in-

18. Carolyn Merchant has described one dimension of modern subjectivity as the scientist who interrogates, even tortures, nature so as to extract its secrets and bounty. She quotes Francis Bacon (*De Dignitate*): "For like as a man's disposition is never well known or proved till he be crossed, nor Proteus ever changed shapes till he was *straitened* and *held fast*, so nature exhibits herself more clearly under the *trials* and *vexations* of art [mechanical devices] than when left to herself" (*The Death of Nature: Women, Ecology and the Scientific Revolution* [San Francisco: Harper, 1980], 169; emphasis original). Rather than being the servants of creation described in Genesis 2, humans are now narrated as the masters of a feminine, constrained, slavelike nature. Pierre Manent, in his examination of modern political thought, speaks similarly when he casts the gospel of Hobbes, Locke, and Rousseau as, "In the beginning, the world was without form and void, without laws, arts, or sciences, and the spirit of man moved over the darkness" (in *The City of Man* [Princeton: Princeton University Press, 1998], 183). Modern humanity has become historical, which means it flees God, nature, tradition, and

structive, however, is the extent to which several postmodern critiques of subjectivity are attuned to, and help illuminate, the formal dynamics of the Genesis story as described by Bonhoeffer. Jean-Luc Nancy, for instance, writes, "The question [i.e., who comes after the subject?] therefore bears upon the critique or deconstruction of interiority, of self-presence, of consciousness, of mastery, of the individual or collective property of an essence."[19] Nancy's reading of the modern philosophical tradition, a tradition he thinks summarized by Hegel, posits a subject that appropriates to itself, in apriori and (given modern technological powers) practical fashion, a world of exteriority and strangeness. Modernity moves according to a metaphysical picture of Being as appropriation. Others, to use theological language, do not signify as a grace received. Instead, they appear as things waiting to be appropriated by us. This tradition needs deconstructing because it unleashes so much violence in the world. In place of an appropriating subject, Nancy asks if we might envision a "someone" who is not master of itself and others but instead "comes indefinitely to itself, never stops coming, arriving," thereby suggesting an identity marked by openness to a genuine other, a genuine limit (*WCAS*, 7).

In similar fashion, Michel Henry reflected upon the barbaric, technological character of modern culture.[20] "Technology consists in the unconditional subjugation of the Whole of being, which becomes the Object, to man, who becomes the Subject—the Object of the Subject, then, disposed before him and disposed of by him, at his disposal therefore, having no other end than this being at the disposal of, subject to tallage and corvée as the serf of this new Lord" (*WCAS*, 158). For Henry it is Kant who best summarized the modern Subject as the transcendental self that appropriates all beings to itself through various acts

established law. This flight is a form of constant rebellion in which the only acceptable law is the (arbitrary) law the human being gives to itself.

19. Jean-Luc Nancy, introduction to *Who Comes after the Subject?*, ed. Eduardo Cadava, Peter Connor, and Jean-Luc Nancy (New York: Routledge, 1991), 4. Hereafter cited in text as *WCAS*.

20. In his 1987 book *Barbarism* (repr., London: Continuum, 2012), Henry argued that the scientism and technophilia of modernity made it impossible to appreciate, and thus also nurture, the distinctiveness of life (as compared to mere existence). By reducing all creatures to their material surface, culture would all but inevitably become nihilistic and turn against life.

of representation: "For the subject is nothing other than this: that which in making appearances appear, in this same gesture, makes be everything that is" (*WCAS*, 163). To re-present others is to bring them within a horizon of meaning and significance that is determined at the outset. Henry insists that there is dishonesty and deception involved here because this subject, though perhaps thinking itself responsible for the appearing/signifying of all others, cannot bring about its own existence. The subject that actually exists in its world does not exist as the result of its own representation of itself. What is needed, thought Henry, is a way of characterizing the post-Subject as "someone" appearing in an *ek*-static movement—a coming from beyond that is also a witnessing to the transcendence of others—that takes him or her beyond the security and sameness of representational consciousness.

This postmodern desire to open the self to the one who is genuinely other was further reflected in Jean-Luc Marion's response to Nancy's question. In "L'Interloqué" Marion offered an analysis of an encounter with a genuinely other person, an encounter in which the other's sanctity is acknowledged. In this encounter the subject's self-mastery is destabilized and decentered by a claim that is made. When one is met by and spoken to by another, the first appropriate response is "This is me!" It is a response made without the mastery or confidence normally assumed by the modern subject because now I must be attuned to how my actions may or may not violate another's integrity. "I experience myself being claimed, that is, called upon in the accusative—interpellated as suspect and not as subject, named in the accusative and therefore dispossessed of any nominative function. The interpellated *me* marks the absence of any constituting *I*, under the—in this respect, totalitarian—authority of the claim" (*WCAS*, 243). For Marion, the claim of the other upon me spells the "disaster" of the autonomous, world-establishing I.[21] Rather than being free

21. Jean-Louis Chrétien's description of the "call and response" structure of human existence is an important supplement to Marion's account of the *interloqué*. Before we speak we are always already called by and joined to another. "We speak for having heard. Every voice, hearing without cease, bears many voices within itself because there is no first voice" (*The Call and the Response*, trans. Anne A. Davenport [New York: Fordham University Press, 2004], 1). Insofar

to appropriate the world at will, the I that is met by another must pause and allow itself to be questioned by that other to determine if he or she has been made the victim of the I's neglect or violence.

Nancy, Henry, and Marion each worry about the modern self's desire to secure itself and the world in terms established by itself. As autarchic and autonomous, this self is not genuinely open to or receptive of a genuine other. It acknowledges no limit at the center of its life. It can perceive limit only (temporarily) at the margins, and as a reality to be overcome.

If we return to the Genesis story, we can make the argument that modernity's rejection of limit is ultimately a rejection of God. Why? Because the rejection of limit and need is also a rejection of God as the one who establishes the sanctity of each creature and who provides for our need. To acknowledge God is to appreciate that we cannot live from out of ourselves. It is to affirm that each creature that exists is the expression of a divine love that desires all creatures to attain the fullness of their being. To be modern is to reject limits and to install oneself as a god.

Consider Eve's encounter with the serpent, who asks, "Did God say, 'You shall not eat from any tree in the garden'?" (Gen. 3:1). Bonhoeffer has no interest in assigning blame to the woman. Nor does he think it fruitful to ask where the serpent comes from (the Bible, he says, does not aim to explain something like the origin of evil). What he focuses on is the new, decisive possibility that the serpent's question raised within the human being: "Through this question the idea is suggested to the human being of going behind the word of God and now providing it with a human basis—a human understanding of the essential nature of God" (*CF*, 106). For Adam and Eve the serpent's question becomes a "godless question" not because it is a question *per se*, as if questions were impermissible, but because Adam and Eve now place themselves in the position where they are the judges over how questions are to be answered.

---

as our response is constituted by love, "Our task is not to give an answer that would in some sense erase the initial provocation by corresponding to it, but to offer ourselves up as such in response, without assigning in advance any limit to the gift" (13).

There are questions that are in the service of loving and learning. But there are also questions that aim to establish the self as the authority by which others are to be judged and understood. Bonhoeffer thinks that the encounter with the serpent brings about this latter kind of questioning and response. Adam and Eve do not respond by saying "Here am I," thereby opening themselves to the other. They, in essence, assented to the serpent's question, "Did God say?," thereby establishing themselves in a position of power and mastery. Rather than submitting to God's word, they exalt themselves to a position *sicut deus* ("like god"), and now live in open rebellion against God. "Humankind is now *sicut deus*. It now lives out of its own resources, creates its own life, is its own creator; it no longer needs the Creator. . . . Adam is no longer a creature. Adam has torn himself away from his creatureliness" (*CF*, 115).

For Bonhoeffer the authentic human creature is the one who accepts life as an interdependent membership with others, and as a grace that comes from beyond the power of human knowing and manipulation. For Marion the *interloqué* is the one addressed (in German, *der Angesprochene*) and claimed by another. Several features of the *interloqué* bear noting: this self is not autonomous because it is always already compelled to be in relation;[22] this self lives through surprise rather than through itself; and this self is always subject to the judgment of the other. "The *interloqué* provides the beginning—the most basic, hence the first, determination—that abolishes the subject: selfhood is initially wounded by the very fact that, before the self can constitute itself, the claim has already exiled it outside its 'mineness.' The wound that originally tears selfhood obscurely manifests the origin itself—the *interloqué*. Before ever knowing by what or by whom, the *I* surprises itself, as *interloqué*, and has always done so" (*WCAS*, 244–45).

Nancy, Henry, and Marion present critiques that, in various ways, characterize modern subjectivity as an imperial, totalizing presence in the world. In the work of annexing and appropriating the world—what Bonhoeffer described as humanity's sinful rebellion against creatureliness—others are repeatedly violated.

22. Berry observes, "There is, in practice, no such thing as autonomy. Practically, there is only a distinction between responsible and irresponsible dependence" (*Unsettling of America*, 111).

Though continuously active, this is a self that, according to Emmanuel Levinas, is nonetheless "asleep" (might we not also say, following Bonhoeffer, "dead"?) because it is not alive and responsive to another in its singularity and transcendence.[23] For Levinas "the very life of the human" is in the unsettling of the mastery of the self in the approach of a genuinely transcendent other who calls and inspires the self to a life of responsibility.

Embracing Creatureliness

The Genesis story we have been following indicates that human creatureliness is worked out in care and companionship, rather than arrogance and appropriation. It is now important to see why our creaturely vocation cannot be worked out alone.

Besides inviting the *'adam* to take care of fellow creatures by "tilling and keeping" the garden, God says, "It is not good that the man should be alone; I will make him a helper as his partner" (Gen. 2:18). Bonhoeffer observes that elsewhere in the Bible God alone is designated as a partner and help to human beings. We should, therefore, be astounded that animals, perhaps because sharing the same soil-based body and divinely breathed vitality, are presented to Adam as potentially fulfilling this position. "At the point where God wishes to create for the human being, in the form of another creature, the help that God is as God—this is where the animals are first created and named and set in their place" (*CF*, 97). Adam names the animals, thereby establishing a relationship with them, but none of these relationships attain a level of a genuine partner and helper.[24] Why this is so we are not told.

23. Levinas asks, "Isn't the liveliness of life excessiveness, a rupture of the containing by the uncontainable, a form that ceases to be its proper content already offering itself in the guise of experience—an awakening to consciousness in which the consciousness of awakening is not the truth, an awakening that remains a first movement—a first movement toward the other of which the intersubjective reduction reveals the traumatism, secretly striking the very subjectivity of the subject? Transcendence" (*WCAS*, 215). Answering his own question with "transcendence," Levinas makes clear that the fundamental question is how to live in the face of limit without transgressing and appropriating it. Genuine life is excessiveness and amazement before what comes to me from beyond myself.

24. Bonhoeffer succumbs, incorrectly in my view, to a history of interpretation in which the naming of animals is equated with mastery over them. He says

God then causes a deep sleep to come over Adam, during which time God removes a rib and creates another human creature from it. This creature is presented to Adam, who calls her woman (*ishshah*) because she comes physically from him (*ish*) and is, he says, "bone of my bones and flesh of my flesh" (2:23). According to Bonhoeffer it is significant that this woman is created while Adam is asleep, because this reinforces that she exceeds his expectations and preparation. Though fashioned from his flesh, the woman is decidedly neither an extension of him nor the result of his decision. She is a limit, a creature with its own integrity that emerges out of the darkness of sleep. "That Eve is derived from Adam is a cause not for pride, but for particular gratitude, with Adam. Adam does not infer from it any claim for himself; instead Adam knows that he is bound in a wholly new way to this Eve who is derived from him. This bond is best described in the expression: he now belongs to her, because she belongs to him" (*CF*, 97). Though the woman is clearly a limit to Adam, she and he exist in a needful and necessary relation to each other, a relationship described as mutual belonging and the sharing of one flesh. The two do not merge or blend into each other so as to abolish their individual creaturely identities. The belonging that characterizes their life together is based precisely on their being different from each other.

Mutual belonging and the companionship it makes possible reveal a profoundly important way of living with limit. This way of living Bonhoeffer calls love. Prior to the creation of the woman, Adam related to limits with the understanding that they were to be received as God's gracious gifts. Adam thereby received the gift of the other with faith and gratitude, but not yet with love. "The Creator knows that this free life as a creature can be

of the animals, "They remained a strange world to Adam; indeed they remain, for all their nature as siblings, creatures subjected to, named by, and ruled over by, Adam" (*CF*, 96–97). Clearly there are forms of naming that do establish hierarchies and systems of domination, but the biblical text does not in the first instance warrant this interpretation. Adam's naming takes place before sin has entered into and distorted relationships. It makes more sense to say that naming makes possible relationships the precise character of which is yet to be determined. Naming one way or another simply lays out different ways of relating to others (for example, naming a plant a "fruit," a "flower," or a "weed" evokes different responses within us).

borne within its limit only if it is loved. . . . The helper who is a partner had to be at once the embodiment of Adam's limit and the object of Adam's love. Indeed love for the woman was now to be the human being's very life (in the deepest sense of the word)" (*CF*, 98).

The woman is for Adam a unique other or limit because she is made from his body and so is intimately related to him. This intimacy, however, entails a reciprocal love by her for him because she knows herself to be drawn from him, indeed carries his body within her. The reciprocal love of the man and woman is foundational because it makes possible a life that can bear limits. It is love that will keep the human creature from transgressing, violating, and appropriating another because it is love that enables the lover to make room for the beloved to be itself. Love is the hospitable disposition that creates the space and the freedom for another to be. Without love there is the danger that the other will be perceived as a threat or as something to be hated. When this happens, shame enters the world.[25]

Erazim Kohák has shown that the love and belonging that characterize the relationship between Adam and Eve are not confined to the human realm. Living on the land, patiently and with affectionate regard for it, gradually produces the sense that just as the land belongs to us, we also belong to it. (It is not insignificant that agrarian traditions describe the bond between human beings and the land and its creatures by using the marital language of "husbandry.") Eating food grown on one's place, heating oneself by its energy, allowing oneself to be inspired by its potential and beauty—all occasions that join our flesh to the flesh of the world so that it can rightly be said that we become "one flesh" with it—reveal a fundamental deception in all claims to possess land outright.

25. Bonhoeffer describes shame as expressing the fact "that we no longer accept the other as God's gift but instead are consumed with an obsessive desire for the other. . . . Shame is a cover in which I hide myself from the other because of my own evil and the other person's evil, that is, because of the dividedness that has come between us" (*CF*, 101). One can compare Levinas in this regard, who describes shame as the freedom that has become murderous (*Totality and Infinity: An Essay on Exteriority*, trans. Alphonso Lingis [Pittsburgh: Duquesne University Press, 1969], 83–84).

Kohák argues that the concept of possession operates at a formal level that often denies the life-giving bonds that exist between us. "The bond of belonging that grows up over years of life, love, and labor is the most basic truth of being human in a world."[26] Labor, rather than simply contributing to an accumulation of land understood as private capital (as John Locke thought), leads to an appreciation of the sanctity and grace of the world insofar as this labor is inspired and directed by love. To say that another belongs to me is not to make a possessive claim. It is, rather, to indicate that without him, her, or it my life would be diminished. This is why Kohák continues by saying, "The living truth of having is belonging, the bond of love and respect which grows between one being and another in the course of seasons. The claim to having is as strong as all the love and care a person gives, and only that strong. It is crucial to have no more than we can love, for without love the claim to having becomes void. Loveless having, possessing in the purest sense, remains illegitimate, a theft."[27] Recognizing the other's value and integrity is, therefore, always also an invitation to commit to this other's well-being.

After describing the man and the woman's life as the love of mutual belonging and becoming one flesh, Scripture adds, "And the man and his wife were both naked, and were not ashamed" (Gen. 2:25). Bonhoeffer interprets their nakedness to mean their innocence before, and their obedience to, each other. In their primordial state the man and woman do not face each other with fear, remorse, or as a threat, because their life together is one in which the integrity of each other is affirmed and served. "Where one person accepts the other as the helper who is a partner given by God, where one is content with understanding-oneself-as-derived-from and destined-for-the-other, in belonging-to-the-other, there human beings are not ashamed" (*CF*, 101).

The ultimate meaning of nakedness is to be found in the act of self-offering to another, an offering in which nothing is hidden

26. Erazim Kohák, *The Embers and the Stars: A Philosophical Inquiry into the Moral Sense of Nature* (Chicago: University of Chicago Press, 1984), 107.

27. Ibid., 107–8.

from the other and nothing is kept for oneself except insofar as it might be shared. That people were created naked is a sign that we were called to live before each other in postures of welcome and nurture. To stand naked before another is to communicate the end of agendas that manipulate and control. Once shame appears, however, and once the pornographic desire to objectify and control the other takes hold, it can be overcome only by the forgiveness that restores unity and communion with others. Forgiveness acts as a kind of disrobing or "unclothing" that removes suspicion, hatred, envy, and alienation, and restores people to a reconciled condition in which they can stand before others without shame.[28]

Bonhoeffer's interpretation of this story shows that creatureliness is not something to be endured, perhaps only temporarily (and while awaiting escape to some otherworldly heaven).[29] We can say this because creaturely life at its most profound realization leads to the loving embrace of the other, an embrace that does not stifle or diminish others but instead nurtures them to more fully become themselves. In our belonging to, and service of, others, love is revealed as the hospitable gesture that gratefully receives and nurtures what has been received (even one's own body), and then offers and shares it with others. Human creaturely life, life that is without shame, makes possible a self that can relate to others in such a way that its life—what it needs, desires, and enjoys in life—makes no sense apart from the belonging and fellowship of life *together*. The human creature that comes before and after the modern subject is a person who lives in welcome and in service of others.

28. Bonhoeffer develops this theme in *Ethics*, ed. Clifford Green, trans. Reinhard Krauss, Charles C. West, and Douglas W. Stott (Minneapolis: Fortress, 2005), 306–7.

29. In *Letters and Papers from Prison*, ed. John W. De Gruchy, trans. Isabel Best et al. (Minneapolis: Fortress, 2009), Bonhoeffer wrote,

> One only learns to have faith by living in the full this-worldliness of life. If one has completely renounced making something of oneself . . . then one throws oneself completely into the arms of God, and this is what I call this-worldliness: living fully in the midst of life's tasks, questions, successes and failures, experiences and perplexities—then one takes seriously no longer one's own sufferings but rather the sufferings of God in the world. Then one stays awake with Christ in Gethsemane. And I think this is faith; this is *metanoia*. And this is how one becomes a human being, a Christian. (486)

Eating Our Way into Creatureliness

Having outlined the contours of human creaturely identity, we can now turn to some of the practical implications that follow from this account. Responses to Nancy's question, "Who comes after the Subject?" showed that we cannot think about human identity without also thinking about human propriety, or about how we "fit" and comport ourselves within the world. To ask about *who* we are is also to ask about *how* we are to live where we are. The question of "who?," in other words, is not theorized in the abstract. It is worked out and discovered in economic and social patterns of life practiced in the world.

As Nancy and colleagues examined the records of modernity, they saw humanity's inability to fit harmoniously within a world of others. Violence, exploitation, appropriation, and neglect—these were the patterns of life made evident in histories of war, colonialism, sexism, fascism, and ecocide. Had they been attuned to the analyses of Bonhoeffer, they might have concluded with him that we have yet to appreciate and implement the sort of relationships that respect, serve, and cherish the mystery and the grace that others are. The desire to be autonomous and autarchic, the decision to live from out of oneself, appropriating the world at will—all movements characterized by Bonhoeffer as the desire to be *sicut deus*—have led to an unrelenting violation of others and the steady, systemic degradation of the world.

We should pause for a moment so I can be clear about what I mean by "world." Reading Nancy, Henry, Marion, and Bonhoeffer, one can see that they are preoccupied with the social world, a highly urbanized world at that. When they speak of a limit to the self and an opening to the other, they are almost always referring to a personal other. What has been overlooked by them, and by vast stretches of our philosophical and theological histories, is the sense of limit that is fundamental to a breathing, eating, and drinking body. Whereas social limits refer us to political structures and *de jure* forms of dependence, embodied and ecological limits point us to *de facto* forms of dependence that are fundamental, necessary, and inescapable. Of course, political structures quickly shape the forms ecological relationships take (consider the various ways property and land management have been configured across time). But in overlooking the material world of creation we will end up with an impoverished understanding of human creatureliness and creaturely responsibilities. It is no accident, I would argue, that the myopic focus by philosophers and theologians on strictly inter- and intra-human affairs has led to degraded fields, forests, waters, and sky. To conclude this chapter I will, therefore, briefly develop how the production and consumption of food provide an ideal window into the embodied and practical requirements of creaturely life.

Eating is that most intimate act whereby we witness to our need of and dependence on others. Every time we take a bite we demonstrate that we cannot live alone but must continually receive the gifts of another's life. This can be a terrifying realization, particularly when we appreciate that the consumption of another's life most often presupposes another's death. All eating, even vegetarian eating, is an immersion into the complex and mysterious world of fertility, a world in which life and death intermingle with each other to produce yet more life.[30] If we are to eat well, therefore, we must consider which ways of producing and consuming food best honor and nurture the gift that food is.

Given the idolatrous ethos of modernity we have so far described, we should not be surprised to learn that today's industrial food systems presuppose the degradation of fields, plants, animals, and agricultural workers. Given the general ill health of today's industrial diet—laced with fat, sugar, salt, cholesterol, preservatives, and artificial flavorings—we could even say that this system despises eaters. To see what I mean, consider what is believed by many to be a showcase example of "successful" agricultural technique: a vast field of corn.

Corn has long been a staple crop in several of the world's food economies. More recently, however, it has been produced and processed to make a variety of products ranging from sweeteners to diapers to automobile fuel.[31] To grow the massive quantities

30. In *Food and Faith: A Theology of Eating* (New York: Cambridge University Press, 2011), I explore the place and significance of death in the membership of life.

31. In *The Omnivore's Dilemma: A Natural History of Four Meals* (New York: Penguin, 2006), Michael Pollan gives a concise account of how corn emerged as the paradigmatic example of industrial agriculture. For a lucid description of

of corn needed to fuel people, livestock, and cars, vast fields are put into monoculture production. That means land, rather than being the site of diverse forms of growth, is made to grow one crop, often year after year. This "unnatural" form of production creates real challenges for fertility and pest management. On the one hand, corn is a nutrient-hungry plant. If soil is to grow corn year after year, farmers must feed the soil. This has been done with the steady application of fossil-fuel-based fertilizers. On the other hand, fields of monoculture are an open invitation to pests to come and eat. To deal with these pests, farmers must apply a steady stream of poisons to keep them at bay. As soil is degraded and pests and weeds become immune to pesticides, the ready option is to apply fertilizers again and again and to use more toxic types of poisons.

This is a situation in which, as we have already heard Wes Jackson say, soil is hammered to death and then put on life support.[32] The application of all these chemicals, many of them highly poisonous, is slowly killing our lands and our waters. Their steady application is filtering into our ground, entering our watersheds, and then depositing in oceans where massive fish-asphyxiating "dead zones" are being created. And so we come to the realization that an industrial approach to making our fields as productive as possible must unleash a diet of chemicals that often have a deadly effect. Food production, rather than being a source of nurture and fertility, is here implicated in the ways of life's degradation.

A complex history lies behind the development of industrial agriculture, a development most often associated with the Green Revolution. Following World War II, it was apparent to many that crop yields needed to increase dramatically if the world's growing population was to be fed. To accomplish this feat new seed varieties were developed, more fields were

---

the industrialization of agriculture in America, see Deborah Fitzgerald's *Every Farm a Factory: The Industrial Ideal in American Agriculture* (New Haven: Yale University Press, 2003).

32. See Wes Jackson, *Consulting the Genius of the Place: An Ecological Approach to a New Agriculture* (Berkeley: Counterpoint, 2010), for a statement and plan for a new agriculture not based on monoculture production. Jackson, a geneticist and founder of the Land Institute (based in Salina, Kansas), has been developing perennial crops grown in polycultures as a way of combatting the loss of soil fertility and the proliferation of pests.

opened up to agricultural production, underground aquifers were pumped and rivers dammed, animals were taken off the land and put in confinement, land was consolidated into the hands of fewer owners, and agricultural work came to be performed by machines and migrant workers. Massive agricultural corporations presided over these developments, providing the contracts, seeds, fertilizers, herbicides, machine implements, and processing necessary to bring food to market. To many people the Green Revolution was and is an unqualified success. Norman Borlaug, the figure most associated with the Green Revolution, was awarded the Nobel Peace Prize. He had saved millions from starvation.

A growing number of people now wonder if the Green Revolution has been properly named. Is it "green," or perhaps "brown," owing to the fact that industrial agriculture depends from beginning to end on the massive consumption of oil? How sustainable, really, is a form of agriculture that, as we have already said, is premised on the degradation of land and water (we should add to this list the abuse of millions of chickens, pigs, and cattle in confinement, and the degradation of farmworkers, who often labor in unsafe conditions without adequate compensation or worker benefits)? How just is an agricultural system that deprives common people of access to land, and instead enriches large (often absentee) landholders and corporations? The mark of global, industrial agriculture is that food's production, rather than being understood as an ecological reality, and therefore performed according to the limits and potential of land and animal, is made to submit to the economic demands of efficiency, transportability, storability, and profit maximization. Nutrition and health have been eclipsed in this economic calculus.[33]

It would be a mistake to vilify farmers caught up in industrial modes of production, especially when we recognize the enormous economic pressures and the highly unpredictable factors of weather, disease, markets, and trade agreements they regularly face. Consumers often demand that food be cheap, convenient, cool, and copiously available. If the processing and

33. In *The End of Food* (Boston: Houghton Mifflin, 2008), Paul Roberts writes about how the reduction of food to an economic reality now imperils the viability of fisheries and agricultural systems around the globe.

packaging of foods is an accurate indicator, they also want food shorn of all connection with dirt, struggle, blood, or death. What consumers do not appreciate is that having this kind of food means that land, water, plants, livestock, and people will be abused. The care of each other takes time and skill. It presupposes communities in which the skills of husbandry are learned and refined to meet the specific needs of each place. In a cutthroat, fast-moving, bottom-line-conscious economic environment, there isn't enough time for such affection.

Is not the reduction of agriculture to an industrial system, and of food to a commodity, a clear contemporary manifestation of our rebellion against our creaturely condition? As consumers we have come to believe that we can eat our way through the world without the skills of attention and care. Having grown to despise manual labor and agricultural work, we have become—the Food Network notwithstanding—the most ignorant and reckless eaters the world has ever known. It is as though we want to be little food gods upon the earth, with the world's cornucopia cheaply and conveniently available on demand.

What would a creaturely approach to food look like, and what would it practically entail? We would need to begin with the realization that food is first and foremost a gift from God given for the nurture of the world. Though it clearly functions within human economies, and so falls within monetary considerations, *food is God's love made delectable*. There is a world of difference between naming food a commodity or fuel and naming it God's love made delectable. If food is the latter, then it is the perpetual invitation into a life of hospitality and sharing and fellowship. When food is properly produced and received, those who come within its field of nurture are refreshed and equipped to better become themselves. When eating is inspired and informed by Jesus as the one who called himself the "bread of life," then food eaten around a table becomes an entry point into a eucharistic life that heals and feeds and reconciles the whole membership of creation.[34]

Lest you think these are merely pious sentiments, consider the difference this disposition makes in the life of a chicken.

34. I develop the notion of what I call eucharistic table manners in *Food and Faith*, chap. 5.

Today's industrial chicken lives a life of misery. If it is a broiler, and thus intended for meat production, it has been genetically engineered to grow to slaughter weight in close to half the normal time. Rapid weight gain puts this chicken in considerable physiological stress, rendering the bird incapable of regular movement. But that is not a problem since it lives in confinement, surrounded by thousands of other similarly stressed birds. If the chicken is an egg layer, approximately eight to ten birds will be confined in a wire cage roughly the size of a filing cabinet drawer (imagine the chicken having to live within the space of roughly a sheet of paper), which is stacked on top of other such drawer-sized cages. These, again, are highly stressful conditions, as excrement from above rains steadily upon them. These birds need to be debeaked so that they don't cannibalize or peck each other to death.[35]

Chickens do not need to be raised this way. They shouldn't be raised this way because, to put it simply, chickens are not meant to live in confinement conditions like these. To realize their full potential, what we might describe as their God-given chickenness, they need to be free to move about, search for grubs and insects, and then nest in a secure place. When farmers receive chickens as gifts from God, they will see that their task is to live in a hospitable relationship with them, a relationship in which the nurture, protection, and happiness of chickens is the primary concern.

A growing number of consumers and farmers are now realizing the cruelty and inhumanity of much of today's meat production and processing.[36] They are responding to the need to grow food more responsibly and with less destructive effect by getting smaller and opting out of the industrial complex that requires the use of expensive inputs and poisons: growth hormones, antibiotics, and toxic chemicals. Being smaller, they can be more attentive and careful with the life that is entrusted to them. They can take the time to learn from ecological processes

35. For a detailed account of the industrialization of chicken production, see Steve Striffler, *Chicken: The Dangerous Transformation of America's Favorite Food* (New Haven: Yale University Press, 2005).

36. For a detailed, and painful, exposé of the cruelty in today's slaughtering facilities, see Timothy Pachirat, *Every Twelve Seconds: Industrialized Slaughter and the Politics of Sight* (New Haven: Yale University Press, 2011).

and species interactions to see how farming can be a more harmonious, self-healing, fertility-generating affair. This means that the chickens they provide will be more expensive. That is how it should be, given the fact that farmers have rarely been fairly compensated for their work, and given the fact that industrial-trained eaters consume too much meat.

Mine is not an argument for expensive food. It is, rather, a plea that we learn to be honest in our food pricing, and recognize that we are nowhere near something like full-cost accounting when it comes to the production of food. All eaters need to understand that behind today's relatively inexpensive food there are a variety of hidden or unnoticed costs that are deeply unjust, costs like the following: chronic disease (type 2 diabetes, hypertension, high cholesterol, cardiovascular disease) directly correlated to an unhealthy diet; wasted water and eroded/degraded soil; exploitation of agricultural workers and food service providers; loss of food democracy and food sovereignty (the idea that farmers and consumers determine appropriate food production for their families and communities) around the world; the piracy and patenting of life forms by major corporations; the privatization of water; the accumulation of greenhouse gases in our atmosphere; and the scandal of nearly one billion inadequately nourished people.[37] The argument that we are doing poor people a favor by providing them cheap food loses its luster when we acknowledge that it is precisely the poor around the world who bear a disproportionate share of the above injustices.

I am well aware that there are many people who can hardly afford the relatively inexpensive food already available. Put in elevator-speech form, what I am advocating for is a new food politics in which the government subsidies that now go to industrial producers be shifted to small-scale farmers who treat fields and livestock and workers with greater respect. I am asking that

37. There is a growing literature on these injustices. I recommend starting with *Manifestos on the Future of Food and Seed* (Cambridge, MA: South End Press, 2007), edited by Vandana Shiva, along with Shiva's own *Stolen Harvest: The Hijacking of the Global Food Supply* (Cambridge, MA: South End Press, 2000); Robert Gottlieb and Anupama Joshi, *Food Justice* (Cambridge, MA: MIT Press, 2010); and Jean Ziegler, *Betting on Famine: Why the World Still Goes Hungry* (New York: New Press, 2013).

a larger group of food consumers, many of whom are spending less of their monthly income on food than any generation in history, recognize the full costs of their eating and pay more, as they can, to support a better agriculture. I am asking for a Farm Bill that supports the production of real food rather than the commodities that enrich agricultural corporations. I am asking that politicians and planners attend to the racism behind the creation of "food deserts" and "food swamps" that leave people in urban areas and rural communities without access to fresh food and consign them to shopping at gas stations, fast-food outlets, and convenience stores. I am asking that health-care providers and hospital administrators demand the production of good food as a necessary step on the way to the promotion of a healthy society. I am asking teachers to develop curricula, field trips, and service-learning projects that will teach children that food comes from the land rather than a factory or store. I am asking citizens that they demand from their politicians food economies that connect eaters with local producers wherever and whenever possible. I am asking eaters that they take more time to consider where their food is coming from, learn the histories behind food products, and then seek out buying options that are healthy and humane.

I am especially asking Christians that they learn to appreciate eating as being of the highest theological significance, and one of the most practical ways to show that they have committed to extending God's hospitable presence in the world. For too long too many Christians have believed that God's primary concern is the fate of their individual soul. This drastic reduction of the sphere of God's activity needs to be expanded to include the whole scope of creation, because that is where God is daily at work. Jesus's ministries of feeding and healing show that God is in the food business. It is time for churches to join with God in the work of the production of good food and the promotion of fellowship and conviviality.

If Christians and their churches take this task seriously, many possibilities come into view.[38] To start, many churches own land

38. For a description of some of these possibilities, see Fred Bahnson, *Soil and Sacrament: A Spiritual Memoir of Food and Faith* (New York: Simon & Schuster, 2013); Fred Bahnson and Norman Wirzba, *Making Peace with the Land: God's Call to Reconcile with Creation* (Downers Grove, IL: InterVarsity, 2012); Rachel Marie Stone, *Eat with Joy: Redeeming God's Gift of Food* (Downers Grove, IL:

and house large kitchens. Could these lands not be converted to grow food and flowers for parishioners and the community around? Could these kitchens not be put to neighborly use, teaching people the arts of preparing and preserving food grown with their own hands? If gardening work is indeed work that introduces us to God's ways of being with the world, then churches should seek out opportunities for parishioners to get their hands in the soil, caring for the creatures that God so clearly loves. They should profile the skills of gardening and cooking work as vital to their own faith development.

Community Supported Agriculture (CSA) is one of the growing sectors in today's food economy. In this system, consumers partner with area farmers by committing to buy shares for a season. Consumers benefit by receiving a weekly box of fresh food containing whatever is in season and is produced by the farmer. Farmers benefit by receiving payment up front and knowing that they will have eaters for what they produce. In this arrangement the risks and the benefits of food production are shared.

What would it look like to implement a system like Church Supported Agriculture? In this system, specific congregations, or a collection of congregations, can partner with farmers so that both benefit. More than simply a buying club, such a system will enable these congregations to arrange to bring parishioners to the farm so that they can see with greater clarity and honesty the fragility and freshness of life, and the demands of care.[39] Participating in farmwork, they may even come to appreciate the kinds of faith formation that happen while one is seeding, weeding, treating a sick animal, and gathering in a harvest. Churches could also come to understand the financial pressures farmers face in the purchase of land and in the production of food, and then perhaps provide financial backing and support. What if the "mission field" came also to be understood as an actual agricultural field? I don't think this is a stretch. Farming

InterVarsity, 2013); L. Shannon Jung, *Food for Life: The Spirituality and Ethics of Eating* (Minneapolis: Fortress, 2004); and Jennifer R. Ayres, *Good Food: Grounded Practical Theology* (Waco: Baylor University Press, 2013).

39. In *Fair Food: Growing a Healthy, Sustainable Food System for All* (New York: Public Affairs, 2011), Oran B. Hesterman discusses the value of buying clubs, along with many other ways consumers can help develop a better food system.

that honors God and creatures is a powerful countercultural witness to a system bent on degrading the sources of life.

No doubt, many more possibilities exist for Christians to become involved in the healthy production and the hospitable sharing of food, including things like the sponsorship of farmers' markets and neighborhood gardens, leadership in food advisory committees and school lunch programs, and advocacy on behalf of farmworkers and food providers. The range of what can happen will vary from place to place because each community has its own unique potential and set of challenges. The key is to start paying attention to the mundane act of eating, and then discover in it ways of being and practices of faith that promote the nurture, and the healing, and the reconciliation of the world.

The scriptural witness is clear: the scope of God's reconciling ways has never been confined to the human realm. What God seeks is the reconciliation of all things, "whether on earth or in heaven" (Col. 1:20). Insofar as Christians commit, through their eating, to be a reconciling presence in the world, they may yet learn to be agents of the "good news" that Paul says has been proclaimed "to every creature under heaven" (Col. 1:23). Doing that, they will, perhaps, learn to assume their creaturely identity.

5

Giving Thanks

> Thanksgiving is the experience of paradise. . . . [Paradise is] the *beginning* and the *end*, to which is oriented and through which is defined and determined the entire life of man and in him all of creation.
>
> Alexander Schmemann, *The Eucharist*

> The expression of gratitude is indifferent to all expectations of symmetry or equivalence. It is a blooming, a supplement—just like language when it becomes . . . song in lyrical celebration. . . . The debt of gratitude thus lies at the outer limit of debt. It indicates a festive relationship that remains within the realm of desire—the intense desire to express the joy that is experienced. If it is a reply, it is outside agonistic duality, as if the giver receives while giving, as if the source of the gesture preexisted both of them and originated from an earlier overabundance, a generosity of life obscurely felt to be the very truth of life itself.
>
> Marcel Hénaff, *The Price of Truth*

Giving thanks is the most fundamental and honest expression of what it means to be a human being, because it is here, in the thanksgiving act, that people appreciate and attempt to live into the knowledge that life is a gift.

But thanksgiving, if it is to have much depth or transformative effect, is not automatic. It follows from a detailed consideration of the many ways in which life's nurture, protection, and (potential) conviviality follow from the blessings of God and others. When we take the time to pay close and detailed attention, it becomes evident that the blessings are so numerous in extent and deep in their significance that our offering of thanks resembles an act of faith, and is a testimony to and confirmation of our bewilderment and awe in the face of a world that exceeds our attempts at comprehension. How could we ever express an adequate thank-you for the many gifts—some of them appreciated, but many of them unknown or barely noticed—that come our way?

Genuine thanksgiving leads to human fulfillment because it is in this action that people share, however imperfectly, in the Sabbath rest and delight that marks the climax of creation: they learn to see that creaturely life is the material manifestation of God's love, and as such is to be cherished and celebrated. The inability to express gratitude is, therefore, a clear sign that one's own life, and the life of fellow creatures, are in a diminished or degraded state, a state in which the love of God is hidden or denied. Put another way, to be genuinely grateful is to experience the world as the place of God's blessing and to participate in life's fullness and abundance. It is to bear witness to the salvation life that Jesus makes possible, and to join in God's work of reconciling to himself "all things in heaven and on earth" (Col. 1:16), and thus also to share in the divine love that is making all creatures new (Isa. 65:17 and 2 Cor. 5:17).

But how to be thankful in a world that is clearly lacerated by wounds and in the grip of so much suffering and pain? Would it not be cruel to rejoice in the face of the sadness and misery that surround us?

The expression of thanksgiving has rarely been an easy matter. Sometimes this is because calamities befall us, things like natural disasters or disease, calamities over which we have little control and which we have great difficulty understanding. It is hard to be thankful when we see people recently made refugees by an earthquake, or visit loved ones ravaged by Alzheimer's disease. In contexts like these, frustration and anger seem the more appropriate responses.

A more common and mundane obstacle to thanksgiving, however, is to be found in the habits of inattention and neglect, and in the patterns of ambition and arrogance that daily damage the world. How can we be thankful when in the stress and speed of life we hardly take the time to notice, let alone patiently appreciate, nurture, and protect the miracles of life going on all around us? More deeply, how should we come to terms with the knowledge that the life we are called to celebrate is so readily degraded by us?

As we have already seen, people tend to be idolatrous beings. Rather than seeking ways to nurture creatures into the fullness of their lives—remembering that it is in the disciplines of nurture that we come close enough to perceive the love of God working to be realized in them—people are on paths that redirect and remake fellow creatures to serve alien ends. When engaged in an idolatrous manner, creatures appear, as if by default, in ways that veil their divine intention and thwart their potential. Creatures cannot fully be the blessing they are meant to be because the divine love that inspires and sustains them has been captured by us and made to serve ends that we desire. It isn't that people are usually or intentionally mean-spirited in their treatment of others. But simply by pursuing the well-respected and highly encouraged aims of their peers—Make something of yourself! Get ahead!—they are nonetheless contributing to the frustration of creatures and the undoing of the world, what the apostle Paul called creation's futility and bondage to decay (Rom. 8:20–21).

If we are to move into a position where genuine thanksgiving can become life's accompaniment, what the anthropologist and philosopher Marcel Hénaff calls life's blooming, we must first take some time to consider how the ideals and practical patterns of a culture can get in the way, perhaps even occlude the possibility, of giving thanks. Understanding that, we can then better consider the steps that will lead us into thanksgiving, what Alexander Schmemann called "the experience of paradise."

Rejecting Gratitude in Modernity

Insofar as scholars are paying much attention to the phenomenon of gratitude—which is not very often—it is not uncommon to find them saying that modernity is, in various ways, premised on its rejection. To be modern is to reject the old, embrace the new and the "now" (from the Latin *modo*), and look to the future. Unlike traditions that honored and cultivated the knowledge and customs of the past as an inheritance to be gratefully received and continued, in modernity people sought liberation from previous cultural forms, increasingly characterizing them as confining, backward, and oppressive. As Louis Dupré put it, "Anxious to assert its superiority to past epochs, its culture exchanged the older claim of upholding a tradition for the one of surpassing it."[1] It is counterproductive to the spirit and the aims of progress to be grateful for past traditions and present communities that are presented as being impediments to the life we want now and into the future.

The general philosophical sentiment just described had incredible practical power and a wide reach into the various domains of politics, economy, education, and the arts. Following Peter Leithart, we can say that something like a "methodological ingratitude" had come to dominate the modern imagination. Forms of public life were no longer to be conducted as if people were the beneficiaries of gifts, since that would smack of the traditions of patronage and obligation that governed traditional societies. To be modern is to be autonomous, a law unto oneself. It is to dare to make history by fashioning worlds that express what we desire. To be grateful would be to acknowledge one's need of and dependence upon others. It would be to suggest that we cannot stand on our own.

1. Louis Dupré, *Passage to Modernity: An Essay on the Hermeneutics of Nature and Culture* (New Haven: Yale University Press, 1993), 145. Dupré is careful to note that the rejection of the authority of past traditions does not mean that history disappears from the human imagination. Instead, the meaning of history shifts from being the source of normativity to being the arena in which people explore the possibilities they might imagine. "Whenever human action shapes the future, the idea of history as indefinite progress logically follows. But to render progress acceptable the new must justify itself before the authority of the past or invalidate that authority altogether" (152).

The sixteenth century witnessed a wide-ranging disruption of traditional patterns of reciprocity. The old religious forms of gift and gratitude were disrupted by the Reformation, the rise of cities and powerful princes, and the development of a military technology that chipped away at medieval politics of gift. The rise of a monetary economy recalibrated the balance of gifts and commerce in European economic life. The proliferation of written contracts was a sign that it was no longer possible to depend on traditional forms of obligation.[2]

It is important not to underestimate the psychic upheaval these developments represent. Consider that before this time it was customary to see ingratitude as a monstrous vice that assaulted the flourishing of life.[3] Why? Because acts of gratitude functioned as a bonding power or social glue that enabled people to recognize and live into their responsibilities to each other. Practices of giving thanks communicated one's dependence on others to make it through life. To forget or forsake the responsibilities and the kindnesses that accompany an appreciation of how people benefit each other is to become worse than a beast. 

None of this is to say that before modernity social life was all pleasantries and light, or that the perceived importance of gratitude rendered all relationships a joy. Gratitude is difficult because the bonds to others that are a benefit can also be experienced as a burden or an impediment to personal flourishing (especially when the bonds we live through are not permeated by a spirit of love). Gratitude is crucial to the life of a culture, because when people give thanks for others and for circumstances, they *remember* the contexts of interdependent

2. Peter Leithart, *Gratitude: An Intellectual History* (Waco: Baylor University Press, 2014), 112.

3. Leithart continues: "It was a Renaissance truism that ingratitude was irrational, monstrous, unnatural, and unjust, a vice and fount of further evils, which could lead only to murder, theft, adultery, robbery, resentment, and vengeance" (112–13). Margaret Visser, in her history of the practices of thanksgiving across cultures, observes that "ingratitude is the worst sin because, as a movement of sheer rejection, it accompanies the preliminary fracture, and then goes on to encourage further breakage. A maxim of Publilius Syrus became, in sixteenth-century English, 'We have named all the naughtiness that can be objected when we have termed a man unthankful'" (*The Gift of Thanks: The Roots and Rituals of Gratitude* [Boston: Houghton Mifflin Harcourt, 2009], 309).

need and help, and they become more inclined to promote relationships that nurture and celebrate a life that is shared. This is why philosophers, when they have talked about gratitude, have said that thanksgiving acts as the moral memory of a community. The flourishing of a society depends on the regular, intentional acknowledgment and celebration of all the (human and nonhuman) members that help a community function.

With the birth of modernity the character of relationships and the sense of one's responsibilities changed. As would become clear in the political philosophies of Thomas Hobbes and John Locke—and then in multiple further variations—for human responsibilities to be legitimate, they must be freely chosen. People do not "naturally" exist in a state where they are dependent on each other. Instead, they are more or less disconnected, self-legislating individuals. Their primary work is not to honor their need of each other but to seek to fulfill their own desires. As Hobbes put it, "No man giveth but with intention of good to himself, because gift is voluntary; and of all voluntary acts, the object is to every man his own good."[4] Though gratitude might have a role in private, familial, and social life, the ordering of political and economic life was to be decided on other, more "rational" and self-interested, grounds. As Adam Smith would famously say in his *Wealth of Nations*, "It is not from the benevolence of the butcher, the brewer, or the baker that we expect our dinner, but from their regard to their own interest. We address ourselves, not to their humanity but to their self-love, and never talk to them of our necessities but of their advantages."[5]

4. *Leviathan* 15, quoted in Leithart, *Gratitude*, 125. Leithart continues by noting that even though Hobbes is an egoist, he is not narrowly self-interested. It is possible to act in ways that are good for others and to be grateful for gifts received. What we see in his work, however, is the functionalization of gratitude: "Gratitude 'greases' the machine of benefits, mutual service, gifts, and acts of kindness that make the world run smoothly" (126).

5. Adam Smith, *Wealth of Nations*, bk. 1, chap. 2. In *Religion and the Rise of Capitalism* (1926; repr., New Brunswick, NJ: Transaction Publishers, 1998), one of the classic treatments of the moral upheaval that modern capitalism created, R. H. Tawney summarizes the shift like this: "The medieval theorist condemned as a sin precisely that effort to achieve a continuous and unlimited increase in material wealth which modern societies applaud as a quality, and the vices for

It would be an enormous task to detail the many ways that ingratitude expresses itself in modernity. What I would like to do, therefore, is show its significance in some aspects of economic life, because it is in the day-to-day sharing, producing, and purchasing of goods and services that we practically work out, affirm or deny, the many memberships—our dependencies on lands, ecosystem processes, and communities—that make life possible. Modern economic practices, as we will see, contribute decisively to new forms of human subjectivity.[6] My specific aim is to indicate briefly the ways in which people's relationships to places, things, and others underwent a profound transformation, a transformation in sensibility and sensitivity that made it much more difficult for people to appreciate, and accept responsibility for, creaturely memberships. Insofar as people lose sight of the significance—and blessing—of creaturely membership, they not only perform the rebellion described by Bonhoeffer as the core movement of "The Fall," but they also render the prospect of genuine thanksgiving difficult and less likely.

We can start with the following observation by Hénaff, who in his magisterial book *The Price of Truth: Gift, Money, and Philosophy* has provided an astute and deeply penetrating account of modern economies and their departure from previous forms of life:

> We may ask if the whole of the enormous movement of the modern economy—what is now a global production machine—might not be the last and most radical way to eliminate the gods, to do away with gift-giving and debt. It may be that we produce, exchange, and consume in order to reduce our relationship to the world and to each other to the management of visible and quantifiable goods, to prevent anything from escaping the calculus of prices and control by the marketplace, so that the very concept of the priceless would disappear. Then nothing would remain outside the realm of commerce. Material innocence would finally have been achieved: no more faults, sin, gift-giving, or forgiveness,

which he reserved his most merciless denunciations were the more refined and subtle of the economic virtues" (35–36).

6. In *The Dismal Science: How Thinking Like an Economist Undermines Community* (Cambridge, MA: Harvard University Press, 2008), Stephen Marglin says, "The assumptions of economics are the assumptions of modernity: economic man is a bare-bones, stripped-down version of modern man" (81).

> nothing other than the mistakes in calculations, positive or negative balance sheets, and payments with agreed deadlines.[7]

Hénaff is describing how in modernity the character of human exchange shifts decisively. Though people have always exchanged goods and services, what they understood themselves to be doing in this activity has not stayed the same. For instance, in many premodern, traditional, and indigenous societies, the exchange of goods was not about accumulation but about the establishment of bonds of recognition and relationship. This is why it was important to place giving and receiving within a ceremonial, rather than simply a commercial, context. "Ceremonial gift exchange manifests a fundamental structure of reciprocity as a condition for all social life in the human species."[8] Giving a gift was not simply about giving back, repaying a debt, or exchanging property. It was, instead, an invitation to establish, continue, and honor a relationship with another who is understood to be a vital member in a shared life:

> The purpose of ceremonial gift exchange is not to be morally sublime through saintly offering but to recognize one another through the back-and-forth circulation of presents, to publicly express the recognition according to rules of deference, and to provide proof of it following conventional forms. The end of the gift is neither the thing given (which captures the attention of economists) nor even the gesture of giving (which fascinates moralists) but the creation or renewal of an alliance. Ceremonial gift exchange is a relationship: a public act without which there is no community; from the perspective of ceremonial gift exchange, to wish for a gift that remains unknown is to wish for the death of reciprocal recognition.[9]

Societies that practice ceremonial gift exchange are distinguished by a felt need to acknowledge and honor the bonds of

7. Marcel Hénaff, *The Price of Truth: Gift, Money, and Philosophy* (Stanford, CA: Stanford University Press, 2010), 20–21. Hénaff's work should be read in conjunction with Karl Polanyi's landmark study *The Great Transformation: The Political and Economic Origins of Our Time* (Boston: Beacon Press, 1944), a study that demonstrates how the modern market economy led to the severing of relationships between people and their lands and communities.

8. Hénaff, *Price of Truth*, 134.

9. Ibid., 141.

interdependence and help that make possible our life together. This is why the refusal of a gift is such an insult: refusal expresses a rejection of the gift and a rejection of the giver. To say "thank you," however, is to affirm the "you" as a vital and appreciated presence in one's life. On the other hand, to give a gift to another and to give thanks for a gift received—these are acts that express one's respect for others and one's desire to be in continuing relationship with them. They even show the commitment of oneself to try to be an abiding and beneficial presence to them. Rather than believing oneself to be capable of living alone and from out of oneself—the temptation Bonhoeffer described as the desire to be *sicut deus*—the ceremonial giving and receiving of gifts signifies the desire to be a communal being (from the Latin *com-munia*, a sharer of gifts [*munia*]), a being that accepts and honors the obligations of a shared life.

A crucial element in cultures that practice gift exchange is the realization that life moves along in the sharing of goods with each other. The desire to possess is the desire to take a gift out of circulation, and thus impede the flow of life. This is why Lewis Hyde, in his influential study *The Gift: Creativity and the Artist in the Modern World*, lays down the following as a cardinal property of a gift: "Whatever we have been given is supposed to be given away again, not kept."[10] To want to possess, and so to eliminate the need for gratitude, is to misrepresent and misunderstand one's place in the world. To be unable to give to others is a sure sign that we want to take ourselves out of the circulation and sharing of things, and thereby short-circuit our development as responsible and grateful beings.[11] The importance of continuity of relationship can be seen in the one who receives thanks when he or she says, "You are welcome." Gift giving and gift receiving are fundamentally about nurturing relationships. To be ungrateful, to be unwilling to give thanks

10. Lewis Hyde, *The Gift: Creativity and the Artist in the Modern World* (New York: Vintage Books, 1979), 4.

11. "Between the time a gift comes to us and the time we pass it along, we suffer gratitude. Moreover, with gifts that are agents of change, it is only when the gift has worked in us, only when we have come up to its level, as it were, that we can give it away again. Passing the gift along is the act of gratitude that finishes the labor. The transformation is not accomplished until we have the power to give the gift on our own terms" (ibid., 60).

and receive it, is to be blind to one's condition of need and blessing, and to be morally obtuse.

Market exchange, the shift from viewing things as gifts to viewing them as commodities, represents a decisive shift in sensibility, because now a person's relationships to others are brokered by markets, merchants, and money. Markets are not, in and of themselves, evil. They are vital to the allocation of resources, the setting of prices, and the pairing of human talents and work to the business of keeping a community functioning and healthy. But markets are not innocent either. In modernity a market ideology developed in which new assumptions about individuals, communities, and land began to dominate. As the Harvard economist Stephen Marglin has noted, modern economists celebrate "the self-interested, calculating individual and the market as the means to realizing individual satisfactions."[12] With this core commitment to self-satisfaction in place, it was all but inevitable that practices that nurture and strengthen communities would wither. "Undermining community is the logical and practical consequence of promoting the [modern] market system."[13]

The appearance of merchants in modern societies is also important to consider because they often came from outside the region and community. They were not known for their fidelity to the community, nor did they need to know deeply the nature of what it was that they were selling. Their value resided in making an increasingly anonymous world available for sale. One of their decisive contributions was to narrate and render the world as a vast storehouse of commodities. In so doing, they contributed to the impersonalization and abstraction of relationships that existed between people and the things they needed. Not being the producers of what they sold, merchants did not need to develop the skills or sensitivities that would lead to sympathy, even affection, for what they sold and for those to whom they sold it. Meanwhile, those purchasing from merchants did not

12. Marglin, *Dismal Science*, 3.

13. Ibid. "Markets, based on voluntary, instrumental, opportunistic relationships, are diametrically opposed to the long-term commitments and obligations that characterize community. By promoting market relationships, economics undermines reciprocity, altruism, and mutual obligation, and therewith the necessity of community" (27).

need to have a direct hand in the production, and thus a deeper and more detailed understanding, of the things they needed. As a result, people would find their knowledge of the world on which they depended greatly simplified. When people are reduced to being consumers of the world, shoppers for the things they need, the conditions are set for an ignorant and negligent relationship to others and the world.[14]

The merchant is also distinguished as a person who trades in money, and money, as Karl Marx well understood, is the great dissimulator: it opens the possibility of boundless powers of acquisition that can be applied to any and every thing. Its indeterminacy means that it can be translated into everything, and be the agency by which all things can be acquired. This is why Marx named money the "pimp" between a person and the means of life. Because money represents the near-magical power of being able to abolish distance, weakness, and stupidity, people who possess it believe they can engage the world however they like.[15] Money, in short, has the potential to create forms of desire that release people from the responsibilities of communal relationships because it represents such power and seemingly unlimited possibility. To have money means to be able to be ignorant, unsympathetic, negligent—even a despiser

14. Today's food economy illustrates precisely this problem. Because people shopping for food do so in an anonymous economy where each item travels hundreds, even thousands, of miles, and because the history of food production and processing is neatly veiled behind attractive packaging and marketing, consumers are in no position to see, let alone fight against, the abusive and unjust practices that punctuate the various links in the food chain.

15. In the manuscripts of 1844 Marx said money is a "visible divinity" that fundamentally transforms personal agency (one's own stupidity or incompetence or infidelity can be overcome with the flash of a bill).

> Being the external, common *medium* and *faculty* for turning an *image* into *reality* and *reality* into a mere *image* . . . *money* transforms the *real essential powers of man and nature* into what are merely abstract conceits and therefore *imperfections*—into tormenting chimeras—just as it transforms *real imperfections and chimeras* . . . into *real powers* and *faculties*. . . . Money, then, appears as this *overturning* power both against the individual and against the bonds of society. . . . It transforms fidelity into infidelity, love into hate, hate into love, virtue into vice, vice into virtue, servant into master, master into servant, idiocy into intelligence, and intelligence into idiocy. ("The Power of Money in Bourgeois Society," in *The Economic and Philosophic Manuscripts of 1844*, trans. Martin Milligan [New York: International Publishers, 1964], 168–69; emphasis original)

of the relationships that in fact make every life possible—and still thrive. With it you can set out on your own and capture the world for yourself. It also has the power to cast a veil over the particularity and the sanctity of things, because what now matters about them is not their integrity or mystery or givenness, but their exchange value. As Seneca in his *Moral Letters to Lucilius* noted in the first century, "We no longer ask what things are but what they cost."

Money's status as a universal translator of everything is well known. What needs emphasis is money's ability to create persons who experience freedom in a new way. In his book *The Philosophy of Money* the German sociologist and philosopher Georg Simmel observed that when people have money they can break with the places and communities in which they live.[16] Insofar as one is a wage laborer who makes money, one can, via contract, enter into whatever relationships are available and affordable.[17] Money thus gives its possessor mobility (it can be used anywhere), substitutability (it can stand in for a subject without the subject being there), and fluidity (it can adjust to all kinds of changing circumstances). In a monetized world, people do not need to develop deep bonds with any place or any person. Not having deep bonds, they are, as if by practical necessity, rendered less likely to discern the integrity or sanctity of things, and to nurture the God-given potential within them. They become less likely to perceive the world around them as a place of gift and blessing. In a monetized world everything is, as Hénaff said, reducible to the management of quantifiable goods and to the calculus of prices. In this world one does not ever need to say sorry or thank you.

In her valuable history of the manners and forms of thanksgiving, Margaret Visser says, "Money explicitly encourages the

16. Georg Simmel, *The Philosophy of Money* (London: Routledge, 1990). Clearly this sort of freedom can be a good thing if the "community" one finds oneself in is stifling and oppressive. I would argue, however, that it has ceased to be a genuine community the moment its members are treated inhospitably.

17. Wage labor is a decisive development on the path to autonomy, because it enables a worker to translate labor into money, which can then be translated into the power that makes available every possible good. As Hénaff observes, this principle was so well understood that in some cases serfs and sharecroppers were prevented from selling the products of their labor, since this would have put them on the path toward emancipation (*Price of Truth*, 337).

discontinuities characteristic of modern life. Paying a price that has been bargained for and agreed on in advance completes a transaction: payment is an ending. It is a 'closed deal,' over and done with and nothing personal. Giving, receiving, and gratefully giving back, on the other hand, are expressions of ongoing personal relationship—a continuity."[18] Money becomes a substitute for need and skill because the one who has it does not have to depend on bonds of affection for help, nor does he or she need to undergo the training that teaches one how to understand and use the world well. Moreover, the one who pays another for a good or service does not need to feel any further obligation to that other because the money has been paid.

Does this mean that we should give up on the use of money altogether? I think not. In some cases it is clearly a good thing for people to be able to use money to escape the oppressive contexts in which they find themselves. Moreover, it is plain to see in our histories that money can do much good in the encouragement and formation of relationships and responsibilities. What it does mean, however, is that we need to stop thinking of money as a neutral or benign instrument. We need to appreciate that a strictly monetary relationship to the things of this world often has the effect of rendering us lazy in and ignorant of the world. Money is a medium and a power that shapes what we expect of the world and how we engage others. More specifically, in the time of modernity, money opens up a world that is now understood as a stockpile or warehouse of commodities awaiting purchase. When money becomes the primary and ubiquitous medium whereby people negotiate their relationships with other people and with things and places, the integrity of others, and our responsibility for them, disappears.

These brief reflections on modern economic forms are enough to help us see that a new kind of person develops in modernity, a person who relates to others more impersonally and without a felt need to honor the social and ecological memberships that he or she is a part of and necessarily lives through. Emancipation isn't simply an abstract, philosophical ideal. It becomes real in economic practices that enable people to rise above the world, ignore limits and responsibilities, and then

18. Visser, *Gift of Thanks*, 323.

act as sovereign beings who simply choose from among the world's many options.

> Money's status as universal translator in exchange is the source of its undeniable power of seduction. It makes life flexible and fluid. It makes the world available. . . . Money virtually opens an unlimited number of choices—that is, of access to goods, pleasures, encounters, professional activities, or adventures. Very few of these will actually be realized, but this is irrelevant since what matters is the openness inherent to cash, from which a sense of freedom arises.[19]

By the time we move into what is called the time of postmodernity, the possibilities for, and the depth of, ingratitude intensify. Think of the market now translated into the world wide web, the merchant realized online as Amazon.com, and money as a series of electronic transfers. Never before has the world been so easily available to our every whim or desire. If others are not exactly as we want them, we can pass them over and pick something else. If something else isn't available, we can simply modify and manipulate what is there until it more nearly resembles the taste we happen to have at the moment. Of course, this is not to say that every use of the web and every deployment of a merchant or money necessarily leads to anonymity and ignorance. What needs noting is that these new forms of economic life make possible, and in some cases clearly encourage, habits of inattention, ignorance, and ingratitude that are destructive of communities and creation.[20]

19. Hénaff, *Price of Truth*, 332. Hénaff quotes from the nineteenth-century French novelist Honoré Balzac, who writes in *Le Père Goriot* of the transformation that happens in a person when he or she has money:

> The instant money comes sliding down into a student's pocket, it is as if some fantastic column sprouts up inside him, and on which he now securely rests. He walks more briskly than before, he feels as if he has a fulcrum on which he can lever anything; his glance is open, direct, his movements are quick; he may have been beaten, yesterday, when he was humble, timid, but tomorrow he'll triumph over the Prime Minister himself. . . . In a word, he who a moment before was a bird that could not fly has suddenly recovered his wings." (Ibid.)

20. In her August 26, 2014, *New York Times* essay, "How Social Media Silences Debate" (http://www.nytimes.com/2014/08/27/upshot/how-social-media-silences-debate.html?ref=technology&_r=2&abt=0002&abg=1), Claire Cain Miller reports

It doesn't take much analysis to see in these unprecedented possibilities a fundamental impatience with, perhaps even dislike of, the world. The practical patterns and the widely shared goals of modern economies, along with the many technologies that facilitate their exercise and dissemination, do not teach us to love the world through acts of patient attention and committed care. Instead they inculcate in us the kind of hubris that renders gratitude obsolete.

> The aim of modernity fulfilled means this: humanly created options that endow ordinary people with entitlements no mortal in history, no matter how exalted, could ever have assumed before. While these entitlements are now limited to a relative and privileged few, this cohort already comprises many millions, shows every indication of expanding, and is, in any case, the source of the global zeitgeist. Members of this cohort either have, or can realistically anticipate, the obliteration of all barriers of time and space, instant access to every text and image ever made, the free exercise of any lifestyle or belief system that does not infringe on the choices of others, custom-made environments, commodities, and experiences in every department of activity, multiple enhancements of mind and body, the eradication of disease, the postponement of death, and the manufacture of their progeny in their own image.
>
> Plus improvements.[21]

Gratitude has been replaced with entitlement. The good that freedom of choice represents has become distorted by economic and social forms of life that occlude the need for deep sympathy and responsibility.

Is Creation a Gift?

If gratitude follows from an appreciation of the world and this life as a gift from God, then it is important to describe what it

---

on studies showing that the use of social media tends to keep people within bubbles of familiarity, and thus apart from those who have different points of view. The internet is contributing to the polarization of society as people tend to stick to those who think and act like themselves. Thanks to Judith Heyhoe for pointing me to this essay.

21. Thomas de Zengotita, *Mediated: How the Media Shapes Your World and the Way You Live in It* (New York: Bloomsbury, 2005), 266.

means to say that creation is a gift. What is a gift? Can a gift be given and received, and if so, how?

According to Jacques Derrida, a gift is a highly problematic, perhaps even impossible, idea: "For there to be gift, it is necessary that the gift not even appear, that it not be perceived or received as a gift."[22] More provocatively still: "The gift does not *exist* and does not *present* itself."[23] On the surface, this seems a strange thing to say. Why does he say it?

Derrida argues that the moment a gift appears and is received within an economy of exchange, it ceases to be a gift. The mark of a pure gift is that it is given without motive and without the expectation of return. If a return is expected, even if the return be so slight as the gift receiver's acknowledgment of and gratitude for the gift, then the gift is not gratuitous but has become oppressive: if the receiver of the gift is obligated to respond with a countergift or countergesture, then the freedom of the gift and the one receiving the gift have been compromised. Because the giving of gifts seems to place those receiving them into cycles of indebtedness, gratuity disappears. Put another way, if a gift is part of an exchange called into being by obligation, guilt, a desire to influence, or payment for services, then it is no longer a gift. Moreover, the moment a gift is identified, it seems to have become something else—a commodity, a prized possession, a trophy, or a reminder of a debt. This is why Derrida says, "For there to be a gift, there must be no reciprocity, return, exchange, countergift, or debt."[24]

Robyn Horner has unpacked the *aporia* (a Greek term describing a puzzle or problem that cannot be solved) that "a gift cannot be given," by noting that giving depends on freedom, the freedom of the giver to give and the freedom of the receiver to receive. If there is compulsion of any kind, then gratuity has disappeared. The gift cancels itself the moment it enters an economy or circle of return. "Economically speaking, the gift simply does not work. It is resistant to calculation, unable to

22. Jacques Derrida, *Given Time: 1. Counterfeit Money*, trans. Peggy Kamuf (Chicago: University of Chicago Press, 1992), 16.

23. Ibid., 15.

24. Ibid., 12.

be fully thought, impossible, a black hole. In Derrida's words, the gift is structured as an aporia."[25]

If a gift "does not work," then it would seem that giving thanks does not work either. "For there to be a gift, not only must the donor or donee not perceive or receive the gift as such, have no consciousness of it, no memory, no recognition; he or she must also forget it right away. . . . This forgetting of the gift must even no longer be forgetting in the sense of repression."[26] It is impossible to be thankful for what has never been perceived or received.

Derrida's account of the aporetic character of gift giving has created a small industry of writing, some of it rather tortured.[27] Rather than rehearse the many positions that have been offered in response, I suggest that we start by probing a fundamental assumption guiding the argument.

Why, for instance, should we accept the account of freedom that undergirds the gift aporia? Is it possible, practically speaking—that is, in terms of an account that takes seriously human embodiment and embroilment within ecosystem processes—to even conceive a creature that is entirely free to give and receive? I think not. Put formally, "to be" is "to be in need" and "to receive."

Descartes's famous dictum "I think, therefore I am" is, from any practical, embodied point of view, impossible. It is not thinking that establishes our being but rather our embeddedness in specific places and our relationships to countless other creatures. This is why his dictum needs to be replaced with "I thank, therefore I am responsible to others."

To be a creature is "to be in relationship," and therefore implicated in the lives and deaths of others. There simply is no such thing as freedom from our entanglement in the lives

25. Robyn Horner, *Rethinking God as Gift: Marion, Derrida, and the Limits of Phenomenology* (New York: Fordham University Press, 2001), 7.

26. Derrida, *Given Time*, 16.

27. The most pertinent contribution is Mark Manolopoulos, *If Creation Is a Gift* (Albany: State University of New York Press, 2009). Manolopoulos summarizes the debate as it has been carried out by Derrida, Jean-Luc Marion, John D. Caputo, Stephen Webb, and Kenneth Schmitz. The book is hampered, however, by a weak theological understanding of creation and a too-willing acceptance of Derrida's framing of the question.

of others. To be sure, sometimes our entanglements can become oppressive, making us rightly want to escape them. The problem, however, is not in the entanglement itself but in the absence of love within it. Indeed, we should ask if the desire to be disentangled and unencumbered is not itself a reflection of the anxiety of membership discussed earlier, and thus already an indication of the failure of conviviality-in-relationship that God desires.[28] Understood in terms of the memberships of creation, giving and receiving are not optional matters. The question is not *if* but *how* we are going to go about receiving and giving.

As I have described it, to be an embodied creature is necessarily to find oneself placed within, nurtured by, and responsible to a world of others who come from beyond our planning or control. It is to appreciate that life is not a possession but a *membership* of receiving, sharing, and offering again. That we eat, drink, and breathe means that we must constantly receive, dimly perceiving that every bite, gulp, and breath implicates us in life-and-death dramas that exceed our best efforts to understand.[29] Though we may call food a "gift," this in no way entails that we have comprehended or exhausted the significance of what we so name.

That we name creation, even life itself, a gift does not mean that we are in a position to fully understand or control what we mean. What we are communicating with gift language, however, is that we do not live alone or from out of ourselves, which is why the language of the gift must always be circumscribed by mercy and humility.[30] In certain respects, we could say that the moment we utter a word of thanks for a gift, we are also, and by necessity, involved in an act of confession, because we have to acknowledge our failures in living out the responsibilities to others that accompany our life together.

28. Lewis Hyde has made a similar observation in a nontheological register: "When gift exchange achieves a convivial communion of spirits, there is no call for liberty; it is only when our attachments become moribund that we long to break them" (*Gift*, 91).

29. I have explored the sense of mystery and awe that accompanies eating in *Food and Faith: A Theology of Eating* (New York: Cambridge University Press, 2011).

30. I discuss the importance of humility in the development of a creaturely identity in "The Touch of Humility: An Invitation to Creatureliness," in *Modern Theology* 24, no. 2 (2008): 225–44.

We are creatures bound to soil and fellow creatures, altogether in need of the grace of life. The person who receives is not, as modern economic theory suggests, a self-possessed consumer negotiating among commodities. To live in creation (as contrasted, for instance, with living in a store or somehow "in" an online retailer) is to presuppose a world defined by need, embodiment, limit, eating, death, pain, beauty, and warmth, a world that moves not as a series of business transactions but as a sphere of mutual belonging and responsiveness, a sphere that is saturated with human impotence and unknowing. To say that creation is a gift is not to say that it is a commodity awaiting purchase or that it is a clearly defined object susceptible to our control. It is, rather, to bear witness to a realm of blessing that constitutes our life but is not comprehended by us, and to indicate one's acceptance, however inadequately understood and realized, of a range of responsibilities that seek to honor and nurture and share the blessings received. To gratefully receive creation as a gift is to commit to live faithfully with other creatures so that mutual flourishing can happen.

To see what I mean, we can return to the creation story in Genesis 2–3, where we learned that Adam needed to learn to live with limits. He needed to understand that limits are good rather than a threat, and that the most authentic realization of creatureliness was demonstrated in his love for another. This love we described as Adam's nakedness before Eve, his offering of himself to her in a posture of openness, shorn of his own agendas, and as an invitation to intimacy. It is appropriate to call this self-offering a form of giving, but we need to see that the context of his offering is born out of vulnerability and the incomprehension of being inspired, informed, fed, and met by countless others. He does not "know" whom he is giving himself to (Eve is not his invention or the object of his control), nor does he have possession of himself. He does not even know if he can offer himself properly and in ways that respect and welcome the sanctity of Eve as the one he is giving himself to. All he can do is try to be a source of nurture, all the while being open to the correction and instruction of others who can reveal to him the justice or impropriety of what he attempts. Insofar as genuine intimacy is achieved, more life will follow.

What Adam glimpses is that he is marked by need—need for breath, need for food, need for companionship, need for help: a fundamental need for life—and that the blessings and the pains, the responsibilities and the meanings of his needs can come to light only as he gives himself to the becoming of one flesh with Eve and one flesh with his nurturing place. Adam's most fundamental and abiding creaturely task is to be a witness to the wide scope of his need. It is to demonstrate with the offering of himself that he lives only because he always already receives.[31] Adam's self-offering is his testimony to a world marked by membership and belonging, but also mercy and forgiveness. His giving is a mark of his desire to honor and serve the memberships of which he is a part.

If this analysis is at all correct, then we can see that the Derridean desire to disentangle the giving and receiving of gifts from all forms of exchange is a disaster. It is, in fact, a fundamental distortion of human life as embodied and implicated in the lives of an incalculable number of fellow creatures. To seek something like a gift's purity is to desire the death of relationship, which is necessarily also the death of life! Here it is helpful to recall the observation of Hénaff:

> What matters most is not the thing exchanged (although it does have some importance and a precise status) but what makes it possible, namely the bond between participants. To reply to a gift is, above all, to proclaim (by respecting the nature of each offering and by giving appropriate goods) that one wishes to maintain or reinforce the relationship, not that one wishes to be released from a debt (when the latter occurs, it is precisely the sign that the interplay of gift exchange has become artificial).[32]

This means that gratitude is first and foremost an acknowledgment that we need others, that we are blessed by them, and that we now want to live in relationship with them in ways that

31. This giving of oneself is not a giving that follows from obligation or debt, because the very idea of debt presupposes a ledger in which credits and debits can be clearly delineated. The depth, breadth, and mystery of creaturely membership exceed what any such ledger could possibly contain. Horner is correct, therefore, to say, "If I give, it can only be because I feel I have been gifted with the capacity to give, not because I feel that I must give back" (*Rethinking God as Gift*, 183).

32. Hénaff, *Price of Truth*, 208–9.

honor them as fellow creatures endowed with the integrity and possibility that is uniquely theirs. Insofar as we lack the appropriate attention and humility, and thereby do injury to the integrity of others, confession and asking for forgiveness will be abiding elements in any expression of gratitude we offer. We can go further and say that insofar as we are beginners in the ways of love, there is no giving of thanks that is not at the same time a request for forgiveness and a petition to be instructed in the ways of love.

The giving of thanks, as we can now see, does not proceed from a subject in full possession of itself. Thanksgiving involves a disorienting of the ego and a dispossession of a self that seeks to grasp for itself the gifts of the world. Giving thanks for another goes hand in hand with the giving of oneself to that other. As such, gratitude entails the enactment of a new kind of freedom, not the freedom that seeks release from our entanglements with others, but instead a freedom that is available to and for others.

It is important to stress the role of forgiveness in the work of gratitude, because without mercy people remain trapped within and paralyzed by the weight of their own wrongdoing. Forgiveness lifts the weight and opens the possibility that people may venture to offer themselves in acts of kindness and hospitality to others, knowing full well that in these acts they may do wrong again, either by imposing on others a plan for life that is of the givers' choosing, by not paying enough attention, by being negligent or oblivious, or by not listening. The hard art is to learn to offer oneself to others in ways that do not harm and do not put them in our debt.

Forgiveness, as the parable of the master/servant in Matthew 18:21–35 shows, releases people from crippling debt and liberates them to experience the fullness of life. Forgiveness makes possible the hospitable love that makes room for another to grow and become itself. To appreciate what this means and what it entails, we can return to the garden of Eden, for it is in gardening work that the practical dimensions and responsibilities of hospitality come into view.

Recall that Adam's gardening work is not simply for the providing of food. By immersing his hands in soil, and by committing himself to the growth and flowering of others, Adam is learning both who he is as a member of creation and how he can best live where he is, that is, in ways that are a blessing rather than a curse to fellow creatures. Remembering that God is the primordial Gardener who creates the world through gardening, Adam, by learning the skills of gardening, is learning to participate in God's life-giving, life-sustaining, life-celebrating ways with the world. God creates by "making room" and by creating the conditions in which others can freely become themselves. The whole of creation can thus be described as a performance in hospitality.[33]

Though gardening is clearly marked by active engagement—soil is prepared, seeds are planted, plants are watered and protected, plots are weeded—gardening is also marked by the gardener's withdrawal and restraint. A gardener cannot simply impose her will upon the garden. She must be attentive, patient, humble, and so learn to attune her desire, her expectations, and her work to the needs of the garden. A gardener, in other words, gives herself to the garden so that the garden can flourish. She performs the sympathy that makes possible a symphony of life.

The pattern for this self-giving, says Rowan Williams, is none other than the Triune, creating God, the God who exists in noncompetitive relationship with creatures:[34] "The God who creates a world of freedom, a world that is itself, is a kenotic God, a self-giving, a self-emptying God whose being is for the other." Insofar as creatures are wise and faithful, they participate in this divine life of self-offering: "To live in wisdom is to live in

33. In "Aspects of a Doctrine of Creation" (in *The Doctrine of Creation: Essays in Dogmatics, History, and Philosophy*, ed. Colin Gunton [Edinburgh: T&T Clark, 1997]), Robert Jenson, drawing on the insight of John of Damascus, develops the theme of creation as the work of a hospitable God making room for others within the Triune life.

34. It is important to stress that God exists in noncompetitive relationship with creatures, that is, in ways that nurture creatures to fully become themselves, because too often people assume that God's creating a world implies God's imposing upon that world a design for how things should be. God is thus construed as the master or supreme controller of everything. This position is a great mistake. God is not a creature like us, which means there can be no competition between us. God's power is not coercive but liberating and nurturing. This is why it can be said that God is glorified in a creature fully becoming itself. Creatures do not have to become small for God to be great.

and by this energy of dispossession and outpouring."[35] Just as God the gardener withdraws to make room for the world, all the while nurturing it, so too, hospitable creatures withdraw to make room for the other as welcome guest, all the while offering nurture and help.

Love as the hospitality that makes room for another is extraordinarily difficult. It is a constant challenge to resist the desire we have to reduce others and the world to the expectations we have of them. To move into the ways of love requires an imagination and set of skills that multiple traditions of thought and work, tuned as they are to control, prediction, possession, and comfort, actively resist. Moreover, recalling the naked vulnerability out of which Adam offered himself to Eve, who today wants to offer him- or herself to a world punctuated by violence and abuse? Recalling the naked Jesus hanging on the cross—Jesus the new Adam, the one who shows us human creatureliness in its fullest and most abundant form—who wants to empty him- or herself to the point of death? The gospel witness puts the matter succinctly: the hope of an individual life rests not in self-containment but in the giving away of oneself. "Very truly, I tell you, unless a grain of wheat falls into the ground and dies, it remains just a single grain; but if it dies, it bears much fruit" (John 12:24).

To acknowledge and engage creation as the place of God's gifts is to find oneself repositioned in the world so as to love it and give oneself to it.

Giving Thanks

If my analysis of the receiving of gifts as so far described is at all accurate, then a case can be made that gratitude will play a vital role in the healing of the world and in the establishment of relationships marked by mutual flourishing and conviviality. Giving thanks is much more than a pious or sentimental verbal gesture. It is, rather, a political and economic act of

35. Rowan Williams, "Creation, Creativity and Creatureliness: The Wisdom of Finite Existence" (lecture, St. Theosevia Centre for Christian Spirituality, Oxford, April 23, 2005, http://www.archbishopofcanterbury.org/articles.php/2106/creation-creativity-and-creatureliness-the-wisdom-of-finite-existence).

revolutionary significance. Why? Because a life of gratitude opens the possibility of a new relationship to the world. Gratitude repositions people in the world so that they can now perceive and engage it in a new way.

To see what I mean by this we should return to Schmemann's remark that "thanksgiving is the experience of paradise." To be in paradise is to be in communion with God as the Giver, Sustainer, and Fulfillment of life, and to be in communion with creatures in such a way as to see and delight in them as the material manifestations of God's love. Gratitude marks our participation in the divine love that moves the universe. How can Schmemann claim any of this? By looking to Jesus, the eternal Word of God incarnate, as the one who shows us in his practical ministries that the life of God—and thus the perfection of all life that is—happens in the feeding, healing, reconciling, exorcising, and befriending of others. To be in the presence of Jesus and to feel the power of the Holy Spirit in one's life is to meet the eternal love that nurtures each creature into the fullness of its life. When this love is fully active and realized in creatures—the moment Scripture (Eph. 1:23 and 4:6) describes as God being all in all, God filling all things—then every creature is a pure delight to behold. That is why Jesus is the source of human joy and thanksgiving.

The history of so much of humanity has clearly not been the experience of paradise. Rather than being surrounded by movements of love, people have instead felt themselves and seen others to be the objects of prey or exploitation or neglect. Formed as we are by the patterns and priorities of today's economic forces, people readily perceive themselves as little more than anonymous pieces within a profit-generating machine.[36] Earth is the place of

36. A central problem with dominant forms of our economic life is that they deny our experience of belonging in a meaningful, valuable world, and therefore also deaden the expectation that life has lasting significance and purpose. What I mean by this can be seen in the witness of persons who describe themselves as "apatheists" rather than theists or atheists. A *USA Today* news story on growing spiritual apathy among Americans quotes Ben Helton, a high school band teacher in Chicago, who says, after considering what modern science teaches about evolutionary psychology, "We might as well be cars. That, to me, makes more sense than believing what you can't see" (Cathy Lynn Grossman, "For Many, 'Losing My Religion' Isn't Just a Song: It's Life," *USA Today*, January 3, 2012, http://usatoday30.usatoday.com/news/religion/story/2011-12-25/religion-god-atheism-so-what/52195274/1). This

competitive struggle for survival. And so, the evidence of many church structures notwithstanding, this is a social and a material world that, practically speaking, is without God.

The question of immediate importance, then, is whether or not it is possible for us to experience this world as a place in which communion with God, and thus also the experience of God's hospitable love, can happen. Can we encounter our planet home in its relationship to the nurturing God who is *for others*, and thus experience it *as creation*?

For Schmemann it is crucial that we not simply attempt to know something *about* God, but rather learn to be in communion with God's life of love. Following John 17:3, where we read that eternal life is to know God and Jesus Christ, Schmemann says that we have spent too much effort amassing information about God (something even the demons are good at) and not enough time moving into a deep relationship with God, a relationship that, by necessity, includes a transformed relationship with fellow creatures now understood to be participants in and witnesses to the ways of divine love. Knowledge as relationship, knowledge as intimacy, is the key: "*Thanksgiving* is the 'sign,' or better still, the presence, joy, fullness, of knowledge of God, i.e., knowledge as meeting, knowledge as communion, knowledge as unity. . . . Knowing God transforms our life into thanksgiving."[37] The experience of paradise is forever unavailable to us apart from our participation in the ways of God's love.

Knowing God transforms our understanding of life, because now we see that this life and this world are saturated by God's love and delight. The world is not a random, pointless accident. It is instead the sphere of God's daily attention and concern. Remembering that the world was created not as an afterthought or out of boredom, but as a blessing, people can now join with God in the cherishing of every created thing. Schmemann says that

> the knowledge that is restored by this thanksgiving is not knowledge about the world, but of the world, for this thanksgiving is

---

view of persons as cars, a view perfectly suited to (and perhaps made inevitable by) a consumeristic world, presupposes that we are fundamentally without value, isolated, and finally incapable of love.

37. Alexander Schmemann, *The Eucharist: Sacrament of the Kingdom*, trans. Paul Kachur (Crestwood, NY: St. Vladimir's Seminary Press, 1987), 176.

> knowledge of God, and by the same token apprehension of the world as God's world. It is knowing not only that everything in the world has its cause in God—which, in the end, 'knowledge about the world' is also capable of—but also that everything in the world and the world itself is a gift of God's love, a revelation by God of his very self, summoning us in everything to know God, through everything to be in communion with God, to possess everything as life in him.[38]

Thanksgiving testifies to a reoriented mind and a converted imagination in which the people and things we meet are sensed with a new depth of meaning and significance. To give thanks means that each thing is no longer simply a material entity susceptible to measurement, manipulation, and possession, but is instead the sensory manifestation of God's desire that it should be and should thrive, and thus worthy of our commitment to participate in its flourishing. An oak tree, for instance, is no longer simply a vertical log containing so many board feet of lumber. It is a vital member of a diverse ecosystem in which a bewildering array of geophysical, biochemical processes are at work so that it, along with other creatures, can flourish. This is what it means to perceive a tree as having its life in God. As the psalmist understands it, in each creature's flourishing, it gives praise to God:

> Praise the LORD from the earth,
> you sea monsters and all deeps,
> fire and hail, snow and frost,
> stormy wind fulfilling his command!
> Mountains and all hills,
> fruit trees and all cedars!
> Wild animals and all cattle,
> creeping things and flying birds!
> (Ps. 148:7–10)

Thanksgiving is closely attuned to praise, because when we praise we express our delight in the goodness of what is there. Seeing the goodness of others, what we might also describe as their beauty and sanctity, has the effect of inspiring people to

38. Ibid., 177.

become creative in the ways they contribute to another's full flowering, which is to say that thanksgiving calls people to a more thoughtful and kind involvement with others. In other words, a life of thanksgiving is also a life in which people are committed to correcting the injustices that disfigure and deny the possibility of convivial relationships.

In the mutual, full flowering of all creatures—a world in which pain and bondage and violence are no more to be found—the life of God as the way of love finds its complete earthly expression. As Dan Hardy and David Ford have put it, "Praise perfects perfection. . . . To recognize worth and to respond to it with praise is to create a new relationship. . . . Thanks is the companion of praise, and shares the same strange logic. Just as praise perfects perfection, so thanks completes what is completed."[39] Insofar as human praise of God is not in sympathetic and harmonious alignment with the praise of all creatures, as when our actions interfere with the flourishing of others, then we should wonder if our praise is genuine and true.

Thanksgiving is not reducible to a pious, verbal gesture. Besides leading us into a transformed understanding of the world as the place of encounter with God's love, the action of giving thanks restores to people their role as eucharistic beings and as priests of creation. In this eucharistic, priestly function, I have in mind the ability of people to receive the world from God, share it with others, and give it back to God as a blessing.[40] Again, we can take our cues from Schmemann, who says that when people bring themselves and the elements of bread and wine (as representative of the whole of the material world) to the

39. Daniel W. Hardy and David F. Ford, *Praising and Knowing God* (Philadelphia: Westminster Press, 1985), 6–7.

> The supreme social benefit of praising God is, however, that it helps in discovering the strongest of objective bonds with others: the link through the reality of God. To praise God as Creator and Father giving himself for everyone through Jesus Christ in the Holy Spirit: that is to route all one's relationships through God, and to open them up to his future for them. Praise actualizes the true relationship between people as well as with God, and it is no accident that in the symbols of heavenly bliss the leading pictures are of feasting and praising. (11)

40. "Blessing is the comprehensive praise and thanksgiving that returns all reality to God, and so lets all be taken up into the spiral of mutual appreciation and delight which is the fulfilment of creation" (ibid., 81).

eucharistic table, and there offer them as gifts to God, they embrace and fulfill our humanity as eucharistic beings: "We were created as *celebrants* of the sacrament of life, of its transformation into life in God, communion with God. . . . Real life is 'eucharist,' a movement of love and adoration to God, the movement in which alone the meaning and the value of all that exists can be revealed and fulfilled."[41] When we offer our praise and thanksgiving to God, we are released from the concerns we have for ourselves and are opened to share in God's desire that all creatures be well. Our release, at least in this life, will be accompanied by personal pain, because the opening of ourselves to others and the world will also lead us more deeply into their wounds. But when we give thanks we also express our commitment to participate in Christ's healing, feeding, reconciling, companion-creating, and celebrating ways with the world.

The action of giving thanks amounts to an awakening of the self to the loveliness of the world. To know that each creature is cherished by God, and to appreciate that the whole of this world exists for the mutual flourishing of all, is to see each thing and everyone in a new light: as beautiful and worthy of life; as the object of God's direct and ever-fresh blessing; as gifted with the opportunity to share in the flowering of life; and as bound up in God's resurrecting future, a future in which all that has been hurt and frustrated will finally be healed and liberated. This is the world in which God delights. It is the world in which God desires to reside eternally. It is the world we are called to love. Thanksgiving is the experience of paradise because in it people are opened to share in the love that creates, sustains, and perfects the whole world. Call it heaven's earthly life.

41. Alexander Schmemann, *For the Life of the World: Sacraments and Orthodoxy* (Crestwood, NY: St. Vladimir's Seminary Press, 1963), 34.

Index

Adam and Eve, 108–10, 113–14, 115–19, 148–49, 150–52
agrarianism, 97, 98–99, 101, 107, 117
asceticism, 87–89, 106
Aristotle, 34, 50
Athanasius, 22, 83–85
Augé, Marc, 63
Ayres, Jennifer, 86, 128

Bacon, Francis, 34, 47, 50, 110
Bahnson, Fred, 86, 127
Balthasar, Hans Urs von, 73–74
Balzac, Honoré, 143
Bauckham, Richard, 16, 46
Baudrillard, Jean, 68
Bauman, Zygmunt, 64
Bell, Daniel, 55
Benson, Bruce Ellis, 51
Berry, Wendell, 4, 25, 44, 69–70, 92, 95, 102, 105, 106, 107
Best, Steven, 65, 68
Bishop, Jeffrey, 14–15, 18
Blake, William, 60, 71
Blowers, Paul, 21–22, 23–24, 73, 77, 88
body, 14–15, 18, 21–23, 88–90, 103, 115, 117, 119, 120
Bonhoeffer, Dietrich, 95, 97, 108–10, 113–19, 120, 136, 138
Borlaug, Norman, 123
Brague, Rémi, 34
Bruno, Giordano, 46–47

Caputo, John D., 146
Carlson, Thomas, 57
Cavanaugh, William, 57, 72
Cézanne, Paul, 60–61, 62, 63, 94
chickens, 124–26
Chrétien, Jean-Louis, 76, 112–13
Christensen, Michael, 81
Christie, Douglas, 93–94
Clement of Alexandria, 81
Climacus, John, 88
colonialism. *See* imperialism
Cooper, David, 104
corn, 121–22
creatureliness, 27, 30, 96–97, 98, 101, 104–5, 107, 108–10, 114, 115, 119, 121, 147, 148, 152
Cronon, William, 37–39, 58

Davis, Ellen, 74, 98, 103
death, 99–100, 109
death of God, 6–13, 153–54
Debord, Guy, 64–66
degradation, 13, 27–29, 55, 84–85, 86, 93, 101, 110, 120, 121, 123, 126, 131, 132
deism, 16
dependence, 101–4, 107, 120, 133–35, 139, 142, 146–49
Derrida, Jacques, 145–46, 149
Descartes, René, 34, 43–44, 50, 146
desire, 56–58, 140–41, 157
discipleship, 86–87, 92. *See also* discipline

discipline, 70, 89, 132
disorientation, 10–13, 63–64, 141–42
Docetism, 80
dualism, 21, 93, 103
Dupré, Louis, 41, 45, 47, 133

Eagleton, Terry, 8–10
eating, 101, 104–5, 109, 117, 120–29, 147–49. *See also* food
ecocatastrophe, 27–29
ecological footprint, 40
Eriugena, Johannes Scotus, 44
eucharist, 22, 24, 124, 156–57

Ficino, Marsilio, 16
fidelity, 69–70
Fitzgerald, Deborah, 122
Florensky, Pavel, 79, 87–88
Foltz, Bruce, 42
food, 17–18, 29, 88, 92, 98, 100, 103, 117, 121–29, 140, 147, 149. *See also* eating
Ford, David, 146
forgiveness, 119, 136, 149–50
Foucault, Michel, 52
freedom, 16, 36, 46–48, 54, 56, 58, 67, 72, 75, 89, 100–101, 108, 117, 141–44, 145–46, 150, 151

gardening, 98–100, 103–5, 128, 150–52. *See also* Genesis 1–3
Gauchet, Marcel, 42
Genesis 1–3, 74–75, 97–98, 101–5, 113–14, 148–49
gift, 1, 3, 5, 10, 26, 49–50, 55, 58–59, 91, 101, 108–9, 116, 121, 124, 125, 131, 133–39, 141, 144–52. *See also* gratitude
gnosticism, 1–2, 21, 23–24, 80, 93
Gottlieb, Robert, 126
gratitude, 29, 45, 76, 107–8, 116, 130–57. *See also* gift
green revolution, 122–23
Gregory of Nyssa, 52
Grossman, Cathy Lynn, 153

Hadot, Pierre, 33, 35
Hardy, Dan, 156
Harrison, Robert Pogue, 64, 99
Hegel, Georg Wilhelm Friedrich, 96, 111
Heidegger, Martin, 43–44, 57
Helton, Ben, 151
Hénaff, Marcel, 130, 132, 136, 143, 149
Henry, Michel, 111–13, 114
Heraclitus, 33
Hesterman, Oran B., 128
Hobbes, Thomas, 110, 135
Holy Spirit, 2, 27, 73, 75, 79, 81–82, 88–89, 92, 153, 156
hooks, bell, 100–101
Hopkins, Gerard Manley, 19
Horner, Robyn, 145–46, 149
hospitality, 75, 77, 88, 119, 124, 150–52
Hyde, Lewis, 138, 147

icons, 59, 63, 71, 76–77, 79–80, 82, 87. *See also* perception: iconic modality of
idolatry, 33, 43, 48–55, 57–59, 68–69, 84–85, 90, 93, 96, 121, 132. *See also* perception
imagination, 3–4, 23, 25, 26–27, 30, 57–58, 133, 152, 155
imperialism, 17, 26–27, 96, 101, 120
incarnation, 22–23, 80, 83, 153
industrial agriculture, 17–18, 121–25
Irenaeus, 23, 75
Isaac the Syrian, 60, 62, 93

Jackson, Wes, 18, 64, 122
Jennings, Willie, 25–27
Jenson, Robert, 151
Jesus of Nazareth, 19–24, 30, 73
  and food, 124, 127
  and gratitude, 131, 154
  and iconic perception, 78–79
  as icon of God, 62–63, 80–83
  and self-giving love, 152
  as Word of God, 82–86, 93, 153
John of Damascus, 79–80, 82, 151
Joshi, Anupama, 126
Jung, L. Shannon, 128

Kant, Immanuel, 111–12
Kellner, Douglas, 65, 68
Kelsey, David, 97, 102
Kohák, Erazim, 6, 117–18

Latour, Bruno, 52–53
Leibniz, Gottfried, 42
Leithart, Peter, 133, 134, 135
Levinas, Emmanuel, 52–54, 115

limits, 108–10, 113, 116–17, 123, 142, 148
Locke, John, 37, 110, 118, 135
Lossky, Vladimir, 81, 82, 86
love, 28–29, 91–93
  asceticism and, 87–88
  divine, 4–5, 75–79, 92–93, 113–14, 124, 131, 152–57
  gratitude and, 131–32, 144, 149–50, 152–57
  iconic perception and, 71–79, 87–88
  idolatry and, 57, 71–74
  reciprocal, 113–14, 116–19, 147–50
  of self, 90, 113–14
  selfless, 92, 116–19, 147–50, 152–57

Macbeth (Shakespeare), 7, 10
machines, 14–18, 35, 50, 59, 92, 123. *See also* technology
Marglin, Stephen, 139
Marion, Jean-Luc, 31, 50–52, 68, 71, 94, 112–13, 114, 120, 146
Manent, Pierre, 110
Manichaeism, 80
Manolopoulos, Mark, 146
Mantzaridēs, Geōrgios I., 81
Marglin, Stephen, 136
Marx, Karl, 96, 140
Maximus the Confessor, 85, 88, 89–93
McCarthy, Cormac, 28–30
McFarland, Ian, 97
Merchant, Carolyn, 17, 46, 110
merchants, 139–41
Merton, Thomas, 89
Mettrie, Julien Offray de La, 14
Miller, Claire Cain, 143
modernity, 8–9, 13–18, 33, 39–40, 43–45, 96, 110–13, 120, 133–44
money, 140–42
Montgomery, David R., 99
Moran, Dermot, 44
Morozov, Evgeny, 66–67
Morton, Timothy, 32
Muir, John, 36

naming, 18–19, 26, 29, 31, 48, 50, 91, 96–97
Nancy, Jean-Luc, 95–96, 111, 113, 114, 120
narration. *See* naming
Nash, Roderick, 38
National Parks system, 37
nature, idea of, 31
  ancient view of, 33–35
  wilderness and, 35–39, 58
need. *See* dependence
Nellas, Panayiotis, 81
Nietzsche, Friedrich, 6–8, 12–13, 52, 96
nominalism, 40–43, 59, 112

objectivity, 52–53
Oelschlaeger, Max, 38
Oliver, Mary, 61–62, 70, 94
ontology, 18, 54, 107. *See also* naming
Ouspensky, Léonid, 76–77, 79, 82

Pachriat, Timothy, 125
passions, 90–91, 93
Paul, apostle, 23, 49, 76, 87, 88, 129, 132
perception, 51–52, 62, 68–69, 70–73, 74–75, 78–79
  iconic modality of, 5, 62–63, 70–73, 76–77, 79–80
  purification of, 87–94
  See also idolatry; Sabbath
Plato, 15, 50
Plumwood, Val, 53
Polanyi, Karl, 137
Pollan, Michael, 121
postmodernity, 143
praise, 155–57
Prometheus, 34
Pseudo-Dionysius, 52

random world, 11, 42–43, 47, 59
reconciliation. *See* salvation
Rees, William, 40
Rhinehart, Rob, 17
Rilke, Rainer Maria, 105
Roberts, Paul, 123
Romantic poets, 36
Rousseau, Jean-Jacques, 110

Sabbath, 75–79, 131
salvation, 2, 14, 21–24, 50, 77, 80–83, 127, 131
  theosis and, 81–82
sanctity, 4, 15, 26, 36, 38, 54–55, 59, 70–71, 86, 110, 112, 113, 118, 141, 148, 155
Schmemann, Alexander, 130, 132, 154–57

Schmitz, Kenneth, 146
Scotus, John Duns, 40
Seneca, 141
Shiva, Vandana, 126
Sierra Club, 36
Simmel, Georg, 141
slavery, 26, 46, 48, 55, 100–101
Smith, Adam, 135
soil, 1–2, 14, 17–18, 51, 98–106, 122, 126, 148, 150–51
spectacle (Debord), 64–66
Speth, James Gustave, 99
Stăniloae, Dumitru, 90
Stoicism, 34, 90
Stone, Rachel Marie, 127
Striffler, Steve, 125
subjectivity, 45–47, 50, 55, 57, 59, 76, 95–96, 110–15, 120, 136, 141–43
Syrus, Publilius, 134

Tawney, R. H., 135
technology, 15–16, 46–47, 55, 66–68, 111, 143–44
Ten Commandments, 48–49
Tertullian, 81
Turner, Frederick Jackson, 38

Visser, Margaret, 134, 141
Vitek, William, 64

Wannenwetsch, Bernd, 56, 58
Ward, Graham, 85
Webb, Stephen, 146
Weinberg, Steven, 11
Widdicombe, Lizzie, 17
William of Ockham, 40–41
Williams, Raymond, 32
Williams, Rowan, 77, 151–152
Wingren, Gustaf, 97
Wirzba, Norman, 24, 76, 86, 106, 121, 124, 127, 147
Wittung, Jeffery, 81
Worster, Donald, 36

Zengotita, Thomas de, 68–69, 144
Ziegler, Jean, 126